From Glory Days

Successful Transitions of Professional Detroit Athletes

by
Kurt A. David

Tanas & Associates, LLC
Farmington, Michigan

Cover photo by Bob Taylor (Taylor Photography)
Major League Baseball trademarks and copyrights are used with permission of Major League Baseball Properties, Inc. Pistons, Red Wings, and Lions logo permission granted.

ISBN: 978-0-615-18052-6

PUBLISHED BY TANAS & ASSOCIATES, LLC.
Farmington, MI.

To Tammie and Emma, whose time I've borrowed in order to complete this book.

Contents

Acknowledgments

There are many people I need to acknowledge as part of this project. Bob Page and Eli Zaret provided insightful support and constructive criticism early on. Mike Ridley supplied great knowledge, as well as many, many laughs. Thanks for the expertise of Ken Ruettgers, founder of Gamesover.org, Bob Taylor of Taylor Photography, Lisa Kokko, Jim Mitchell, and my publicist, Eric Smith of Fast Life Marketing. Special thanks to George Blaha for the fine foreword, Tim McMormick, whose encouragement and connections provided me with a burst of energy late in the game, and Pete Mantyla, who took the time to rough-edit my material. I need to thank the countless family, friends, and colleagues who have encouraged me throughout this process. "That's a neat idea," has held true in my mind, especially on the more difficult days. I'd like to acknowledge the most important people in my life; my lovely wife, Tammie, I couldn't have done this without your support, and my daughter, Emma, whose presence reminds me daily that being a father is the most important job on this earth. I'd also like to posthumously recognize my father, who passed away during this project. Through countless games of HORSE in our backyard he taught me the mental side of sports. (Can you believe that it took me until the latter part of my college career to finally beat him?) I miss him dearly and I'm sorry that he is not around to read this book. He would've loved it.

Of course, I must acknowledge and thank the biggest contributors to this project; the twenty athletes chronicled in this book. The process of interviewing these former athletes was a real treat for me and many fine relationships have developed as a result. You guys truly are the heart of this book!

Foreword

Even the best of our highly skilled athletes have had to push themselves since they were young in order to find a spot on the stage we call professional sports. Each and every one of them can tell you stories about players left behind... Players with as much or more talent who somehow didn't make it for one reason or another. For those who did make it the satisfaction had to be immense. Imagine any of us doing what we do best and doing it at the highest level. It would be difficult, wouldn't it, to worry about what to do next when you've achieved what you've been working toward all your life?

How do you do anything else after you've made it to the Super Bowl of life? These men had to figure it out and they did... Some with ease and some not without a struggle. I know you'll read with great interest these real-life accounts from some of the greatest athletes our city has seen...and some of the most interesting personalities.

You could argue that Ron Kramer is the greatest athlete ever from the state of Michigan, with his football, basketball, and track and field skills. His story is here, and so is the story of arguably the greatest middle linebacker ever, the Lions' one and only number 56, Joe Schmidt. There is the irrepressible Lem Barney, as dynamic and popular and talented off the field as he was on. Then what about super scorer Kelly Tripucka and highflying Greg Kelser, two terrific Pistons TV partners of mine, and tough Ted Lindsay, as fine a man as you'll meet, and Tiger pitching stars Frank Tanana and Dan Petry, and Mr. Grand Slam, the Silver Fox, Jim Northrup? Their stories are all here and so are the stories of Tiger standouts Rick Leach and Roger Mason, and Lions kicking great Eddie Murray and powerful Lions fullback Tom Nowatzke.

Kurt A. David was also able to find sweet shooting former Piston Allan Houston and Eastern Michigan and Piston standout Harvey Marlatt and question them about making the transition to life after pro sports. And there are more Red Wings stars in the book as well...Bill Gadsby, Johnny Wilson, Shawn Burr, and John Ogrodnick, who are all household names in our state.

No book on the transition from professional sports would be complete without the incredible story of Dave Bing. The All-Time Piston great and Hall of Fame inductee later became a true pillar of Detroit's business community and a civic leader as well. His transition makes for great reading.

These stories all come from the hearts of the athletes who went on to make a life for themselves and their families after the games were over. Kurt A. David, who played pro basketball in Europe himself, has woven these stories together into an interesting book that reminds us that these stars had to find another playing field after their playing days were over. Enjoy the reading while getting to know these great athletes even better.

George Blaha
Play-by-Play Broadcaster
Detroit Pistons
Michigan State Spartan Football

Chapter 1
LEM BARNEY

Lem Barney played eleven seasons as a Detroit Lion. In 1967 he was named Rookie of the Year for his efforts as a defensive back and on kick returns. Lem played in seven Pro Bowls, was named All-Pro three times, and in 1992 was enshrined into the NFL Hall of Fame.

Lem Barney was a well-rounded youth as he participated in the band, drama club, glee club, and athletics. Since eight years of age he wanted to be a professional football player but he was discouraged from athletics by his mother because of how often he got injured in the neighborhood games. When mentioning his dream of playing football to others, Lem was often told that he was too slow and that he would get creamed. If only his young critics knew then that this boy from Gulfport, Mississippi would someday be named All-City, All-State, All-America, All-Star, All-Pro, and eventually be inducted into the NFL Hall of Fame, they may have relinquished their previous thoughts and comments sooner.

Remaining true to his dream of playing football, Lem received his first taste of success when he entered 33rd Avenue High School in Gulfport. As a quarterback, safety, and defensive punt return he found his love and passion. He also discovered that this passion could take him places, including a chance to play in college. Unfortunately, racial tension was common during this time and segregation amongst the southern universities was still the norm. As an African-American, his only considerations to play were at colleges attended by other African-Americans. He eventually signed to play quarterback at Jackson State University, who had just won the National Negro Championship the previous season. Under Jackson State coach Rod Paige, who now resides as the current US Secretary of Education in Washington, DC, Lem quickly learned that he was very naïve and only one of the many talented athletes on the team. This was evidenced that year, according to Lem, by the fact that there were thirty-nine other Jackson State players who could run the 100-yard dash in 9.5 seconds or less. Lem also learned that his career as a quarterback would be very short lived, mostly because of a teammate named Benny Crenshaw. "(In my whole football career) I only knew two quarterbacks that when they threw the ball it would whistle… Joe Namath and Benny 'Shotgun' Crenshaw," he exclaimed. Though, his days as a quarterback were numbered, it didn't stop him from working passionately in order to find success at other positions. Initially covering punts and kick-offs, Lem was eventually moved to defensive back and set a conference record of twenty-seven interceptions his sophomore year. This record-breaking performance inspired his Jackson State teammates to give him the nickname "Nitrate," mostly because of his explosive quickness.

In 1967, Lem Barney became a second round draft pick of the Detroit Lions. It would be the highest NFL draft choice out of the state of Mississippi until the likes of Walter Payton and Archie

Manning. Lem was proud of the immediate impact he experienced with the Lions right from his first NFL game. During the first defensive play of his first NFL game, Lem intercepted a pass from longtime friend Bart Starr, and ran it back for a touchdown. "That's something Starr and I still kid about to this day," he said. That same year Lem lead the NFL in interceptions, was voted Rookie of the Year, and even saw time as a punter until the arrival of Herman Weaver. Ultimately, he boasted triple back-to-back-to-back Pro Bowls (seven overall), was voted All-Pro three times, is listed in eight different Halls of Fame, and was named by *The Sporting News* as one of the 100 All-time Greatest NFL Players. His eleven-year career with the Detroit Lions could be the envy of any athlete. "(My) first seven years were joyful," he stated. Lem attributed these good times to the family-type atmosphere created by Lions head coach Joe Schmidt, who had previously played for the Lions as a linebacker. During his seven-year tenure as head coach, Schmidt was inducted into the NFL Hall of Fame in 1973. "A Hall of Fame coach ends up coaching a Hall of Fame back," Lem now dubs it. One of the ways Schmidt created this family type atmosphere was by taking the team to Pete Larcos restaurant following home games, which were held at Tiger Stadium during this time. Lem's joy would turn sour during his last four years with the Lions. "I had four different coaches in four years," he stated. This proved especially difficult because of his belief that the coaches are an extension of parents and the team was an extended family. His mother and father stably raised Lem. They ingrained hard work, discipline, and dedication as part of the family foundation. Over the course of his last four years an internal conflict occurred within Lem as he discovered that the fundamentals ingrained at home were not present with some teammates and the Lions' organization. The destabilization of his football family began to wear on him deeply. Simply put, "(My) love for the game prevented me from continuing. I was fed up," he stated. Thinking seriously and long, he discussed it often with his family and knew that he had their support no matter what the decision, which was extremely important to him. At thirty-two years old, Lem Barney decided to walk away from professional football. "The decision to leave the game was a good decision as I look back at it retrospectively," he shared. "I have no qualms about it whatsoever."

Though saddened and disappointed, Lem understood how fortunate he was to be able to leave the game on his own terms, without being released or injured. He recalls a time when he was nearly forced to leave the game on terms that were not his own. Terms that would be frightening to any professional athlete. During his preparation for an upcoming game against the Cincinnati Bengals Lem learned about an offensive tackle named Rufus Mays. The coaches prepped Lem to look for the moment that the imposing six-foot-nine 285-pound offensive lineman would reverse pivot, meaning he was about to pull and run to the short side to block. As expected, come game time, Rufus reversed and began to pull and block. While lowering the silver and Hawaiian blue helmet that he strapped on for many years, Lem's objective became clear; hit the mammoth offensive tackle low and try to cut him down. The next thing Lem saw was seven familiar faces leaning over him, twenty-five minutes later. "I started opening my eyes (and) it was like a haze, lights, and smoke," he said. Then he heard the team doctor shout for a stretcher and state that he was paralyzed. Hearing this, Lem stubbornly refused to be carried off the field and suddenly reacted. "It was like the angel of the Lord touched me," he said. "And I started flapping like a frog for 10 yards on my back, (yelling) 'I ain't paralyzed.'"

Following a recent CAT scan Lem discovered that he has

probably incurred six or seven concussions throughout his playing career, each suspected from events similar to the one with Rufus Mays when he was knocked out. He understands that he could've been forced to walk away many times from the game and feels fortunate to have had the opportunity to end his career on his own terms. As a result, you'd think that Lem's transition from sports would be easier. He walked away on his terms with his family's support. Despite this appreciation, the emotion of having football as part of his life for over twenty-two years provided a somewhat difficult transition. "The love or the passion (for football) was that great in me," he said. "It took about eighteen years for the love of the game, or the vaccine of the game, or the drug to complete my system where I could sleep without bopping my wife in the mouth or punching her while trying to knock down a pass, or make a tackle (while) dreaming about playing." Eventually, Lem's passion for football subsided and he simply explained, "I woke up one morning and I wasn't gritting my teeth (or) biting my tongue (anymore)."

Lem's current, well-conditioned physique makes it easy to believe that he still works out. "I work out constantly," he stated. "I have a few aches and pains but who doesn't. I feel great; I feel better than I look. No restrictive pain whatsoever." Anyone who knows Lem knows he lives his life with passion. He lists three of his current passions as God, tennis, and working out and has taken his ability to passionately connect with people from on the field to his works for the Lord. Now, as an ordained minister, Lem's involved in ministry and attributes many of his past accomplishments in football to the Lord. "The Lord gave me those (gifts)," he said. "That's why I continue to work my body out, to work the temple." To Lem, working out is a form of worshipping the Lord. "It (my body) has come from Him and one day it's going to return to Him," he exclaimed. In a practical sense, working out has also helped Lem replace his passion for playing in the NFL. His daily ritual is to wake up at the crack of dawn and begin a cardio and weight workout. His physical workout then transcends to a spiritual level as he swaps his treadmill and dumbbells for markers, poster board, and a Bible in order to begin pumping out the foundation for an upcoming sermon or speech. Typically, these materials end up strewn all over the counters of his kitchen. Lem's mental and spiritual capabilities are as solid as his firm physique, which is evident when he begins to rattle the thoughts, quotes, and lessons of an upcoming sermon.

Though passionate about his faith, Lem admitted there was a time in his life that he veered away from his spiritual roots. "I jumped ship like Jonah and was in the belly of the whale," he penitently put.

After twenty-two years of competitive football Lem discovered a void created by the absence of his teammates. His solid ability to connect with them caused him to realize that that is what he missed the most; the comradeship. Currently, Lem has the opportunity to connect with Lion players again, but instead of as a teammate it is as a mentor. "Heroes of the Past Mentoring Heroes of the Future," he calls it. It is a program that matches former players with rookies and has allowed Lem to connect with the likes of Charles Rogers and Kevin Jones. He's not allowed to discuss football with the players he mentors, but does preach the most important advice he feels he could give a young player today. "Get involved," he advises. "Get involved into the community, get involved into a church, and get involved with a school." Lem has often used his celebrity platform to walk his talk. Over the years he has been involved with the NAACP, Focus Hope, Black United Foundations, New Detroit, wheelchair basketball, countless schools in the community, and over twenty-five years with the Special Olympics. "When I have an opportunity to share with (young people), I'm doing a 100-yard dash," he says.

Since football, Lem has worked as a public relations specialist with Michigan Consolidated Gas Company as well as a finance manager at a car dealership owned by former Lions teammate Mel Farr. Being employed outside of football was not totally foreign to him. "Most players during the '60s, '70s, and mid-'80s were required to work (other jobs) to help supplement their income," he said. Lem's parents gave him some sound advice by telling him to save his money. Having done so, he now uses his time to reach out to those less fortunate, which was another lesson learned by watching his parents. "We're only what we are now because of what we were then," he stated.

The works of the Lord and family are now Lem's two acclaimed loves. His son, Lem Barney III, daughter, Latriece, and grandson, Lem Barney IV, are his passion. "The thing I like to do now is bring joy on others," he exclaimed. With his strong passion and an innate ability to connect with people, it is very probable that Lem Barney will have as much success spreading joy, as he did playing football.

Chapter 2
RON KRAMER

Ron Kramer lettered in football, basketball, and track while attending the University of Michigan. He continued to display his extraordinary athleticism by playing ten years in the NFL, including a stint under legendary coach Vince Lombardi, while winning two NFL Championships.

Ron Kramer was a very special athlete in his own right. As a graduate of East Detroit High School he received All-State honors in football, basketball, and track. At the University of Michigan he was reportedly the last player to earn nine letters in three sports. He would have had twelve letters, except for the fact that all athletes were ineligible during their freshman year at that time.

Ron's philosophy as a collegiate student-athlete was quite simple. "We didn't go to college to play ball," he said. "We went to college to at least try to get an education." This belief helped Ron complete his Bachelor of Arts degree within four years and displayed the great discipline for which he was known. "When I went to Michigan I played football, basketball, and ran track," he stated. "For four years I had eight o'clock class every morning, I never missed. I had to go to school between eight and twelve (because) practice was every afternoon, all year," he added. He did more than simply practice and play as a college athlete—he excelled. Often Ron was compared to the likes of Jim Thorpe, a multi-sport athlete from an earlier era, as he led Michigan basketball and football teams in scoring two out of three years. He was voted Most Valuable Player three years standing in basketball, and consensus All-American for football in 1955 and 1956. It has been told that this 230-pound athlete was so talented that on at least one occasion he walked over to a Michigan track meet following spring football drills, and won the high jump. The six-foot-four student-athlete endeared his university so much that the number 87 jersey he wore for football was retired immediately following his senior year.

Possessing this amount of athletic success is normally attributed to great self-discipline that is enhanced by sports, but in Ron Kramer's case those around him primarily modeled his self-discipline long before he ever picked up a ball. "I grew up with a great discipline in me and a great work ethic because my dad worked at the Chevrolet Forge and never missed a day," he stated. "(He) worked in the shop all of his life. My mother worked in the cafeteria of (my) high school. Now how could I miss school," he quipped. "I worked on a farm all summer long. I was disciplined by my father and mother, by my grandfather, my grandparents, my uncles and my aunts, we were such a close family," he added. "We're from this little poh-dunk town out in Kansas. My mother's sister married three of my father's family. My mother's sister married my father's brother and my mother's brother married my father's sister. When we used to go there, it was like having all fathers and mothers," he exclaimed.

The solid work ethic and discipline initiated by Ron's family led to his list of collegiate accomplishments and future opportunity. In 1957, the Green Bay Packers recognized his successful endeavors with a first round draft pick and secured the highly touted player from Michigan. As a tight end for the bottom-rung Packers, Ron suffered a serious leg injury his rookie year that many thought would be career ending. Once again, his work ethic and self-discipline prevailed as he proved that he possessed the grit required to play in the NFL by overcoming this injury. "I played another ten years," he boasted. "I (had to sit) out the 1958 season because I went into the Air Force," he added. However, upon his return to Green Bay in 1959, another key Packer acquisition impacted Ron's life. Newly appointed head coach Vince Lombardi led the lowly team to a third place finish in 1959 and two eventual NFL Championships in 1961 and 1962. The influence of this new coach not only had a positive effect on the team, thus great outcome, but also had a personal effect on Ron. "I had discipline before Vince Lombardi, but he enhanced it," he exclaimed.

With the introduction of television to professional football during this era, fame and fortune soon followed Ron's football successes. "TV has changed everything," he stated. "I was right in the middle of the whole thing. In 1961, the championship game was the first one-million-dollar game in the NFL. We got a big payoff for winning, it was $3,500. It was a lot of money," he exclaimed. "I had a lot of friends who were going into business and their starting salary was $3,500," he said. "I made $20,000 (and) didn't know how to spend all of the money."

Following the Packers' championships, the Associated Press named Ron All-Pro in 1962. He was riding the pinnacle of his professional career, but came to a crossroad in 1964. "I made a decision in my life in 1964," he said. "My (six-year-old) son had lost an eye, my marriage was in a bit of turmoil, and I made a decision to play out my option because I came home to be here in Detroit with my kids. My obligation was with my family, no matter what the consequences would be, whether I retired or whether I got to play with Detroit," he added. The Lions gave up their #1 draft choice in 1965 in order to secure him. Tom Nowatzke, who was a rookie in Detroit that season, stated, "Ron taught me more than the coaches. He was a great guy and a great player," he added. Despite such accolades, Ron's decision to play in Detroit was arguably professional suicide. The marriage he came home to salvage eventually ended and he experienced a coaching mindset far different than Lombardi's. It wasn't until Hall of Fame linebacker Joe Schmidt took over Detroit's reins in 1967 that things would turn around and the Lions finished a respectable third place in their division. Missing three games due to injuries during the course of the season, this year would prove to be Ron's final as a professional football player. "I only believe one thing," he said. "Play until you can't play anymore. Why the hell do you want to get out if you're on top? Screw that, play!" With this philosophy in hand, Ron played until he couldn't play anymore. Referring to his multiple knee injuries and operations, he stated, "Now I'm at seven (surgeries), I don't have any more knees, I have new knees," Ron said.

What helped Ron's transition from football go well was mostly his preparation for this day. "I didn't have a downside," he stated when referring to his exit from football. "I didn't have a downside because I was always prepared for what was going to happen. We went to school to succeed in what we were trying to do after we got out of school," he added. Following Ron's retirement announcement from football, he became an executive with the Paragon Steel Corporation in Detroit, where his hard work eventually promoted him to vice-president by the time he finished his twenty-two years in the business. In addition, he has been a football analyst for WAAM and CKLW radio stations for University of Michigan football games as well as WWJ-TV for the Detroit Lions.

Ron has started and is involved with a multitude of charity golf events, spending much of his time with the National Football Foundation, Special Olympics, the Cancer Society, and Boy's Club of Metro Detroit. "You just get involved with all of these things," he humbly stated. "We have a lot of guys that do this, my friends, my pals, my people that I've always had helping," he added. Though a fierce competitor, Ron remembers his modest roots and enjoys reaching out to those in need. He also enjoys reaching out, shaking hands, and signing autographs as he still does at many football games. Ron recently returned from Ann Arbor and the fiftieth reunion of his University of Michigan football team. "This is all part of retirement, too, if you still partake in the activities with your teammates and things like that," he said. "Green Bay treats you exactly like Michigan," he added. "I go to Green Bay up to five, six, seven times a year. I play in different golf tournaments, I go up there and sign autographs, they bring everybody up there and give you four or five thousand (dollars)," he stated.

Ron appreciates the way certain teams acknowledge the players of his day, but has a different view of the modern-day professional athlete. "Football's gotten just like baseball, maybe more," he exclaimed. "They get a hurt finger and they don't play. We didn't play that way," he added. As someone who played before the onset of facemasks, Ron was conditioned to the physical pain and injuries, and considered them almost second nature. Now, almost forty years after his final NFL season, he experiences the reality of these old injuries. "It's horrible," he exclaims. "I have to take Vicodin. I have to take it when I play golf because you have so much arthritis now."

In addition to his physical pain there is another lingering effect that makes his life more difficult. "First of all, most people who were in professional athletics and in the limelight of our society have very large egos to fulfill," he stated. "I played because I loved the game. I loved to play and of course, you know you walk into some place and someone says, 'That's Ron Kramer,' and we sort of live with that," he added. "All of a sudden that's cut off."

Despite the many trials Ron has experienced throughout his many years of football and thereafter, he has been able to maintain a positive attitude and shared his secret. "I have a clock at home," he stated. "It is a clock that has my voice on it and when it goes off my voice comes on and says, 'Okay, Kramer, it's time to get up, make your bed, and adjust your attitude.' I've never, ever got up and not made my bed or adjust my attitude," he exclaims, once again, displaying the self-discipline that has been ingrained since youth. In addition, Ron has another philosophy that has aided him as well. "I've always done what I had to do, I never considered what I did work, and I still don't," he said. "Whether it was in the hayfield or whether it was in school, I never could consider what I did in my life as work, it was my pleasure," he exclaimed. "Happiness is more important than money, happiness is more important than anything. I'm a kid from the eastside, my dad worked in a shop all of his life, I worked on a farm all summer long. Hell, we didn't have a pot to piss in. It didn't matter, we were happy people," he added. "I got a 130-acre piece of property with a lake on it and a partial farm, cottage, and barn. I've never been happier in my life," he stated. "(And) I have two beautiful children."

Ron shares this happiness as he travels once a week from his farm in Fenton to Ann Arbor in order to deliver crates of apples as a gesture of his appreciation to the university that provided his education and opportunity to play. He now applies the strong work ethic that awarded him countless athletic successes to making appearances, raising money, and simply giving to others. With his busy philanthropic schedule Ron Kramer humorously expressed a thought about his present life. "I'm not retired, I'm just tired," he jests.

Chapter 3
TOM NOWATZKE

Tom Nowatzke was a high school and collegiate All-American. In 1965 he was a first-round draft pick in both the NFL and AFL drafts by the Detroit Lions and New York Jets. After playing in Detroit, Nowatzke completed his eight-year NFL career as a fullback with the Baltimore Colts. As an important weapon in the Colt offensive arsenal he received the Unsung Hero Award following their victory in Super Bowl V.

In life we have an empirical work classification known as blue-collar and white-collar. Beyond this color-coding of shirts symbolic to a workforce lies something not so much discussed but almost as obvious. It is the classification of hands. Typically firm, worn, and wide, the blue-collar hand is quite different than its subtle white-collar counterpart. Years of manual labor assist in the development of strength found in a blue-collar hand and it's representation to the life of the one who possesses it. When it comes to Tom Nowatzke, there is no confusion when defining what classification of hands he holds. His meaty paws and sausage-sized fingers are a poster child for blue-collar hands.

"Size fifteen," he boasts when referring to his finger size.

The athletic honors began for this large-stature man in Michigan City, Indiana, at Elston Senior High School. Prior, Tom attended a small Catholic school, but he began to taste success in sports after transferring to the public senior high. "We had a pretty good basketball team and I was a decorated basketball player," he said. "We only lost three games my senior year and went to the regional. We were Metro State Champions in football my senior year, (only) lost one game. I was High School All-American," he boasted. Tom also received All-State honors two years in a row.

When it came to looking at his options for playing any college sports he responded, "Football was the only one." Excelling as a fullback and kicker, Tom received many college offers. "I was coming to Michigan," he shared, "but they wanted to make me a tight end and I didn't want to do that, so I scratched them off my list. In retrospect, I probably should have done that, played tight end, and played five years longer in the pros. It's easier on the body," he stated. "I had other offers, I could have gone to Illinois, I loved Pete Elliott, and I should have gone there, too. I would've played with (Dick) Butkus as we were the same year, but you don't know that (then)," he added. Tom ultimately decided to stay closer to home and signed with Indiana University. "I went to Indiana because they told me I could play three years," he said. "We had nine fullbacks my freshman year, and when we got down to my sophomore year there was three left, and I won the job."

While at Indiana, Tom didn't simply rely on his past successes. With his blue-collar work ethic in tote it didn't take long to find success at the next level and acquire some impressive honors and awards before departing college. As the team's leading scorer his junior and senior years, Tom was voted Most

Valuable Player as a junior, All Big Ten (Conference) two years in a row, and All-America as a senior. He concluded his college career at Indiana University with the Balfour Award, which is given to the outstanding football player of the season. He was also named one of the top ten men on campus, and was voted as the most outstanding to play against by the University of Oregon in 1965.

Tom's thoughts of playing professional football after college took an interesting twist following his senior year. "I was in the ROTC (Reserved Officers' Training Corps)," he said. "I signed up my junior year to be an officer. (During) the off-season of my junior and senior year I started getting letters from the pros. I was supposed to (attend a ROTC meeting) but I didn't go to the meeting and they called me and I told them I wasn't coming. The commandant there or general of the ROTC called me and said, 'You're going to go to the top of the (Army) draft list if you don't sign these papers.' Vietnam was going on at that point," Tom stated. "I didn't sign up and that's when I started with the pros," he simply put.

Tom found himself high on a draft list, but it wasn't for any military enlistment. In fact, he found himself high on two draft lists, which was a precedent as it was the first double draft of its kind. Tom found himself drafted in the first round by both the Detroit Lions in the NFL and the New York Jets, who were part of the AFL at the time (American Football League). Drafting Tom was so important to the Detroit Lions that they had the late George Plimpton, known for his book and movie *Paper Lion*, reportedly call his name at the NFL draft site when it came to their pick. As their first-round draft choice, both teams were quite serious in acquiring the All-American athlete out of Indiana. "The Jets wanted me and so did Detroit," Tom said. "Both of them were on campus at the same time, they were just watching. They both came over to my (parents') house at different times during Thanksgiving because I was going from there to the Coaches All-American Game (and then) to the *Ed Sullivan Show* with the All-American team," he said. "So I go to (catch) the plane in Chicago and find (NFL scout) Dick Pollard, sitting right next to me. I told Dick that I was meeting with the Jets in New York. As soon as we get off the plane I introduce (people from the Jets) to Dick Pollard. So (the next thing I know) they sneak in between him and we're going down the stairs, out the back, into a limousine with Sonny Werbling, and over to Shea Stadium to meet with Coach Web Ubank." During his tour of the 62,000-seat stadium Tom was adamant about getting back to the hotel. "I told them I've got an hour, and then I got to be back," he stated. "So an hour and a half later, they still got me in a room. I (finally) get back to the hotel room and Bud Erickson from the Lions is sitting on the floor, right in front of my room. It's funny now, but at the time I had no idea. (Bud) said, 'You didn't sign, did you?' I told him no, and he asked if I was still open to sign with Detroit, and I said, 'Yes, I am.'"

Later that night Tom headed out to catch up with the other All-American teammates who were on this trip. "So I go, I'm late to dinner, and (Dick) Butkus and (Gale) Sayers are there and as I'm talking to Butkus he asks, 'Are you going to sign with New York?' and I said no. He wasn't either. The next day, the Jets traded Butkus to Denver hoping he'd sign with them and not Chicago and that's when the Jets drafted Joe Namath No. 1. Dick Butkus and Tom were No. 1 to Chicago and Detroit in the draft (and I went to the Lions), and that's how (the Jets) got Namath," he stated.

When discussing the reason for signing with Detroit Tom said, "I watched the Lions once a year, on Thanksgiving Day, because football was not on TV back then. Going to Detroit seemed much better than a start-up AFL team and Detroit had George Wilson as coach and a lot of good players like Karras, McCord, Schmidt, Morrall to win with," he mentioned with a smile.

After leading the Lions in rushing and scoring in 1967, the following year would prove to be difficult as tragedy hit during Tom's fourth year with the Lions. "I broke my neck," he stated while pointing to the middle of his neck. "I crushed the fourth and fifth vertebrae right here." Speaking about the demise that would shortly follow, he elaborated by saying, "My fourth year, we were 9-4-1 and Joe (Schmidt) called and wanted me to switch to linebacker and be captain of the special teams. I said I would do that, so I switched positions." Tom's fifth year with the Lions would be his final. "So I was the last cut and without a job for about ten days," he said. "I called a bunch of teams, I really wanted to play." His wish to play came true when the Baltimore Colts picked him up, but with certain stipulations. "The deal was I was supposed to be tight end, or running back, or a linebacker—(based on) whoever got hurt first," he shared. "It was a one-year deal but it had lots of incentives in it. I started the last eleven games and that was the year we won the Super Bowl. From the shithouse to the penthouse," he frankly put. That season was highlighted with an off-tackle touchdown run in Super Bowl V, for which he received the Unsung Hero Award. Tom would spend two more years with the Colts before being traded from his proclaimed penthouse. "They traded Bill Curry and me to Houston," he said. "So I went down there and after eight years (of playing pro football) they told me that I had to prove to them I could still play, so I retired."

Despite his release from the Oilers Tom counted his blessings. "I was one of the luckier guys because I had a job," he said. "I had this job where I was selling equipment for Clark

Equipment Company." Having already established himself well during the off-season, Tom could now fully commit to his second career, and he stated, "I went to work full-time selling for Brown Trailer Division. I was the regional sales manager for the Detroit operations." In 1975, the business degree that Tom acquired from Indiana University proved beneficial. "(Clark Equipment) decided to get out of the business and I ended up buying (it)," he said. "They had a great name, great name in business for over thirty years. It was a high when I got the dealership for Great Dane," he added. While he was excited to operate Tom Nowatzke Transport Equipment, which is now called Nowatzke Service Center, in Whitmore Lake, Tom still discovered a void from playing professional football. He faced an emotional reality that most professional athletes face once departing from their athletic craft. "When that first season starts and you're not there," he said sadly. "I had a rude awakening before that because of being with the Lions. You drive home and (you feel like) you don't have anywhere to go. That's a low point," he shared. Tom attempted to draw a parallel to the slim odds he faced those last years of playing. "Lawyers, doctors, any profession; you can call 100 of them in and say, okay, September 1 we're going to have a cut," he said. "We're going to keep two and the rest of you we're going to cut. (That's) a lot of pressure," he explained. "I don't think you miss (the pressure) if you're in that element, (though) you look for it."

Positively, Tom found a way to apply his competitive edge into his current line of work. "You know, I had a meeting the other day and I told the other sales reps present that I feel like I can give my quote and beat you," he exclaimed. "You need to feel that way as a salesman, if you don't, you'll be out of business."

Tom talked about how hard he has worked since football. He also talked about the financial differences between someone from his era and today's NFL players. "I was the number five overall pick," he said. "My signing bonus was $45,000 plus I made $45,000 a year with a two-year guarantee. Ricky Williams was the number five overall pick (in 1999) and made 18 million," he exclaimed.

Currently, Tom is a member of the NFL Alumni National Board of Directors and President of the Detroit Chapter. In 1986, he was inducted into the State of Indiana's Hall of Fame and in 1995, he became a member of Indiana University's Hall of Fame. In 2006, he was listed on a College Football Hall of Fame ballot, but has yet to be inducted.

To this day, Tom is still recognized and acclaimed for his football honors, but has not forgotten the blue-collar work ethic that projected him to this position. Despite his large physical stature and many accolades, Tom is not afraid to bend a knee while lending a huge helping hand for a couple of his favorite charities. You can find him in Ann Arbor during the Special Olympics and sitting on the board for the St. Louis Center in Chelsea, Michigan. Tom does not hesitate to attend other charity functions, as well, when it fits into the busy schedule of operating his own business.

Tom Nowatzke's large, weathered hands display the blue-collar effort that has been applied to both football and business. These hands also display a very large Super Bowl ring, size 15 to be exact, which is symbolic of what he still continues to strive for in his everyday life since football...to be a champion in all he does.

Chapter 4
EDDIE MURRAY

Drafted in 1980 by the Detroit Lions, Eddie Murray's NFL career as a place kicker spanned over twenty years. In the Pro-Bowl as a rookie, he would become the first rookie in NFL history to be named Pro-Bowl MVP. Eddie earned a Super Bowl ring in 1994 as a member of the Dallas Cowboys.

Eddie Murray was raised in England for ten years, until the untimely death of his British father. His mother was left with no income and no choice but to move back to her native Victoria, British Columbia. While attending Spectrum High School, Eddie admittedly was a jack-of-all-trades, master of none, when it came to athletics. Excelling primarily at soccer and rugby, he played any chance he could and joined the high school teams as well as participating with local club teams. Eddie played football for a local club, ran track, played volleyball, and was a member of the high school badminton team. Surprisingly, he still found other athletes more involved with sports than he. "As much as that seems, I knew other guys that played other sports that I didn't," he said. "There were some guys who played high school hockey and played club hockey and they were also on the soccer and rugby teams. So to me, it just seems like that's what a lot of us all did. So granted, schedule-wise it was tough. Just so long as it doesn't interfere with your schoolwork," he added.

Eddie lived in an area where hockey was king; therefore, his rugby, football, volleyball, soccer, and track events didn't have a big following. "The biggest crowd I ever played in front of was like 500 people," he stated. After high school, there were no colleges banging down his door, primarily because there was little interest for the sports he played in this area. Other issues compounded Eddie's opportunities as well. "My mother was sick and dying from cancer at the time," he shared. "So dealing with her issues, not having money to go to school, I (just) went to work."

Eddie spent the next year driving a three-ton forklift for one of his friends' father, who owned a local lumberyard. It was while filling construction orders and helping people with weekend projects that an opportunity presented itself to him. The British Columbia Lions of the Canadian Football League held a one-day local development camp. Eddie did well enough at the one-day camp that he was invited to attend a weeklong camp at the BC Lions' stadium in Vancouver. Admittedly, he did not take this opportunity very genuinely and stated, "I used it as a way to get out of work. I really didn't take it serious. So I went to camp thinking, *Hey, this is great. I get to see some of my high school buddies that moved to Vancouver,*" he added.

While trying out, Eddie played wide receiver (which is known as the slot back in the CFL), defensive back, and some backup quarterback. He soon became weary of the two-a-day workouts and stopped showing up for the morning workouts. "I was indulging myself with my friends in the evening and missing morning practice," he shared. This self-indulgent behavior caught up with him by camp's final day during the inter-squad scrimmage. It was clear while playing slot back that the lack of attendance affected his ability to run plays or read coverages. Fortunately, BC Lion's head coach, Cal Murphy, saw through Eddie's cavalier approach to camp and was cognizant of another talent he possessed. Coach Murphy requested that he do some placekicking during halftime of the scrimmage and under the cat-calls and scrutiny of the other 150 camp attendees, Eddie went on to kick field goal after field goal, starting from the 10-yard line all the way to 55-yard line before missing his first kick. Determined, he went on to hit the next two kicks, which made him two for three from 55 yards. The razing by his peers soon erupted into cheering and clapping before Coach Murphy could stop the whole activity and get back to the scrimmage. As fate would have it, this halftime-kicking exhibition changed the course of the rest of Eddie's life.

He was faced with the decision of signing a professional contract, thus lose any opportunity for a college scholarship. The difficulty of this decision was manifested by the fact that Eddie's mother was in her last month of living. "I went back home," he said. Having already lost his father and now faced with the reality of losing his mother, Eddie turned to a major influence in his life, Joe Beckers, who was his high school soccer coach. "I looked up to him not only as a coach but as a father figure," he stated. "I was very close to him. He knew what kind of student I was, which really was not very good in high school." This lack of academic interest would be the deciding factor for Eddie and solidified his choice to attend training camp, where he would be potentially offered $11,000 and a $500 signing bonus.

Fate is sometimes an unpredictable and funny thing and, once again, played a huge role in the direction of Eddie's life. As he was preparing for the BC Lions' training camp a phone call, in fact, a multitude of phone calls offered him another opportunity. Fellow Canadian and Tulane University assistant football coach, Willard Wells, became aware of this young kicking phenom. Knowing that Eddie was about a month away from training camp and potentially signing a professional contract, Coach Wells simply wouldn't take no for an answer to his offer to play for his university. "(He) proceeded to badger the shit out of me," Eddie stated. "He called every day until the day I went to camp. He talked to me for hours, every day. It was, 'Hey, how are you doing? What are you doing? How's your girlfriend? How's your mom doing?' He talked to me about everything every day. He was a great recruiter," Eddie added. Long story, short Eddie agreed to make a campus visit to the university, even though he had no idea where New Orleans was located. "I mean, I didn't know from the forty-ninth parallel below," he laughed. "New Orleans? I don't know where the hell it's at." Eddie's lesson in geography came en route to New Orleans with the assistance of a huge wall map and an elderly lady during a layover at the Seattle airport. It was at that moment that Eddie discovered his destination. His decision to attend Tulane became easy after he was shown the French Quarter, Bourbon Street, and discovered that the drinking age in Louisiana was eighteen years old. "I'm going, I don't even need to see the school, I'm ready to come," he said.

Eddie proved he was ready to attend Tulane by accumulating many honors throughout his time in New Orleans. From 1976–1979, Eddie set nearly every Tulane single-game, season, and career kicking record. He was voted All South Independent Conference four times and two times All-America Honorable Mention.

Despite these accomplishments, Eddie admitted that he

might not be ready to play in the NFL. His confidence would improve after discovering that only one other place kicker was eligible for the NFL draft that year, thus improving his odds to play at the next level. Strangely, Eddie was not getting the normal feelers he expected prior to the NFL draft. He had occasional NFL scouts watch him do a few kicks and a brief workout, but no one was saying anything for sure. While still in New Orleans finishing some classes, Eddie received a call from a hometown friend stating that the CFL's Hamiliton Tigers drafted him in the first round. He received no phone call from the organization, which added to the insecurity that he felt earlier. After two weeks Eddie called the Hamilton front office in order to introduce himself and confirm his first round draft. At that point, they advised him to wait a couple more weeks until the NFL draft before discussing any CFL contract.

Eddie's roller coaster ride into professional football would continue on NFL Draft Day. He and his wife sat at their home in New Orleans with his wife's cousin and NHL player Mike Rogers and his wife. Also present were a handful of Tulane teammates, and a local TV crew who wanted to catch a live moment of his NFL draft. Eddie's ride continued as round after round passed by, while he received promise after promise from the New York Giants that he would be their pick in the next round. This cycle occurred for Eddie through the sixth and final draft round of the day without an official draft. Assured, once again, that he would be the first pick in the seventh round by the Giants, the gang at his house decided to go out and celebrate Eddie's all but certain draft by New York. "We got in (the next day) at three in the morning and went to bed," he said. "At seven in the morning the phone rings and it's (a scout) from the Detroit Lions on the phone." The Detroit scout apparently told Eddie that the Lions were interested in taking him with their first pick of the seventh round later that day. He then went on to ask Eddie about his junior year extra points statistics. "I'm half in the bag and half asleep and I pull out a media guide and tell him what it is," he said. "(Then) I go back to sleep." Five more phone calls from the Lions' personnel followed with requests for one stat after another. "I'm getting pissed because I'm hung over, and I'm tired, and I'm (already) a Giant," he stated. "That's what I kept thinking." By now it was close to the eight a.m. local starting time for the draft and Lions' head coach Monty Clark called to confirm Eddie's imminent draft. Though confused by the roller coaster ride of promises made over the course of the draft, Eddie found himself in good company as the Lions possessed the number one overall draft pick and chose Heisman Trophy winner Billy Sims that same year.

Despite the uncertainty leading up to his draft, Eddie became a solid hit as an NFL kicker. In his first NFL year he was voted to the Pro Bowl and after nailing four field goals during this game, Eddie became the first player in NFL history to be named MVP their rookie season. "My rookie year I made a huge splash," he boasted.

With a phenomenal start, multiple engagements with charitable events in Detroit during the off seasons, and as part of a select few that remained around for off season work outs, Eddie envisioned himself with the Lions forever. However, his vision became blurred at the age of thirty-five when he was let go by Detroit following his twelfth season.

Eddie is still very hurt by this event, not necessarily because of the fact that he was let go, but because of the way the event occurred. "I'm standing there in my jock (prior to practice, on the first day of mini-camp) and one of Coach Fontes's guys says that he wanted to see me," he stated. "I had been captain of the team for a couple of years so I thought maybe he wanted to talk to me about something (in that capacity). So I get dressed and start to go upstairs, and he said, 'No, you should put on your street clothes.' So I knew something was up. I didn't like the feeling of what was going on," he added. "I had heard all of those things said to people who were being cut, so I thought, *Man, I can't believe he's going to cut me.* I went up and I let him (Fontes) talk and he went through 'you've done this, you've done that, you were this, you were that,' I mean, all the (buildup), you know. I always remember he said, 'We're letting you go because we don't want you to (screw) with (newly drafted) Jason (Hanson) at camp.' That's what hurt me," he emotionally stated. "I went from there to basically trying to find a job," he said. "I didn't get an invite to go to camp (with anyone) because it's now after the draft and everybody has made their choice."

Without a job or any apparent prospects, Eddie found himself in professional football limbo. He continued his obsessive workouts and oftentimes equated the workouts to those of a professional baseball pitcher. "I always say, why do you think pitchers go to camp early—because they have to get their arm in shape," he said. "I have to kick to work (my leg) out." Confident that he could still play, Eddie began to receive some inquiries, but discovered they all contained a strange theme. Every inquiry asked about the past debilitating hip injury that he had two years prior. The injury placed him on the injured reserve list for four weeks at that time. Teams that flew him in to try out went so far as CAT scanning his hip. "What I found out when I finally hooked up with a team was that the word was put out, and I don't know by whom but someone at the Lions, stating I was hurt," he sadly mentioned.

Eddie put the past hurt with the Lions aside and focused on one thing, playing professional football. The next seven years of his career proved very fruitful and he humorously gave this phase a title: "Leg for hire," he dubbed it. Initially, slow but once the rumor of a potential hip injury cleared Eddie was given many opportunities to prove his abilities, which is all he asked for. He signed for a week with the Kansas City Chiefs and played in a game against the Steelers. Eddie kicked a 52-yard field goal during this nationally televised game, which provided the exposure he wanted to prove his enduring ability. Two weeks later Eddie found himself in Tampa Bay, where he would remain a Buccaneer for the last seven games of the season. Oddly, this contract came without even a tryout. "Every Tuesday is NFL day off but it's also the day that they bring people (like me) in to work them out," he said. "So I get the call from Tampa Bay and of all things, the day we go down there had to be 50-mile-an-hour winds. I mean, if you're kicking with the wind you're kicking 80-yarders and you can barely make an extra point going into it," he added. With two other kickers vying for the position, the Buccaneers canceled the tryout and signed Eddie. "I was the old guy, so they went to that," he justified.

The following season Eddie was cut by Tampa Bay, but head coach Sam Wyche helped him land a job with the Dallas Cowboys, who had just previously won the Super Bowl. The Cowboys repeated as champions in Super Bowl XXVIII, thus solidifying his ability to still play. Following the Super Bowl wave Eddie found himself eligible for the NFL's new free agency collective bargaining agreement the following season. He became the first free agent signed by the Philadelphia Eagles that year and played the entire 1994 season. Eddie played the entire 1995 season with the Washington Redskins.

The following year Eddie was let go and sat out the entire 1996 season. Approaching forty years of age made waiting for a phone call even more difficult. "I kept myself ready, went to a couple of workouts (but) nothing happened," he stated. "I was contemplating if I wanted to keep doing it, and decided I would so I prepared myself for the following season."

The Minnesota Vikings eventually hired Eddie's leg and he played the remaining twelve games of the 1997 season. After being cut once again, he sat out another entire season. "Now I've made my mind up that I'm going to retire, and I do a one-day signing with the Detroit Lions so I can end a Lion," he said.

Fortunately, finding a job would not be a difficult part of Eddie's transition since he typically worked during the off season his whole career; taking jobs as a manufacturer's representative and even doing commercial loans for a bank. "If I knew I was going to play twenty years I might not have done it," he stated. "But the nature of the beast and the game back then, I could be gone in a week, let alone next year. I mean, your job could be taken away that quickly, there is no guarantee," he added. "I went to work for a tool and die stamping company, and worked out, kicking a little bit. I had a hard time trying to let it go even though I made the decision that I was done." As fate would once again have it for Eddie, his inability to let the game go proved beneficial as he received a call from the Cowboy organization, left his tool and die job, and signed for the four remaining games of the 1999 season. Eddie knew that the Cowboys would not resign him the next season because of the NFL salary cap. Nor would his previous employer rehire him since they didn't like that he quit for the NFL. Shortly after being hired by a friend, he received a call to play once again with the Washington Redskins and finished the final six games of the 2000 season.

"With hopping back and forth, the hiring situation, that whole scenario with the (NFL salary) cap, you know, I didn't mind because I had the temperament to handle it but it became too much," he admits. "I would go right into the season and try to get the timing with the snappers and holders and the team would never get to know me and 'who the hell is this old fart coming in during the season' and all that kind of stuff," he said. "And putting up with all the good and bad of coming in during the season and being ready to go, especially being of the age I was. I was forty-four (years old) in my last year," he shared. "Not only did it start to become a physical challenge but it was becoming a mental (one as well). "I didn't like the music that was played and I didn't like the guys' attitudes and I didn't like the bling-bling, all of that crap was just too much for me. It's a different game now," he exclaimed. "I kept thinking, *What the hell do I have to prove? I played nineteen years, Pro Bowl, Super Bowl, you know. I've got nothing to complain about. If I walk away now I'm content, I'm fine with everything.*"

Eddie had a vivid recollection of the thoughts and events that led to his decision to truly retire. "The last game of the year was Christmas Eve," he stated. "We had to win the last game and get help to make the playoffs. Well, we didn't do our end so we knew we probably didn't make the playoffs. So because of it, my wife says, 'What do you want me to do this week? If you make the playoffs I want to be there because you'll have to stay for Christmas.' And I'm going, look, the likelihood of us making the playoffs are not good. Even though we had a Christmas tree at the apartment I was at we were kind of getting ready for Christmas in both towns. This is ridiculous, (so) I said just stay there (with our daughter), (and) if we make it we'll deal with it," he said. "I was very disheartened about all of the things that were going on, hoping we weren't going to make it. And I thought, *Man, if I'm hoping I don't make the playoffs I don't need to keep playing.* So I had my car packed, jammed up with everything, all my shit, gave my furniture back to the rental people, I mean, I made my mind up we weren't going to make it."

The long drive back to Detroit helped Eddie mentally

transition from football. "I evaluated a lot during that drive," he shared. "What am I going to do? My old football days are just one phase of my life and I'm forty-four (years old). I chose to put my focus in the next phase of my life. You know, I'm not dead and I definitely didn't make the kind of money, I was making portions of good money, I wasn't making a full season. My rookie year I signed for $30,000 a year and when I finished playing in 2000 I was making $30,000 a week," he said. "I just knew that I couldn't keep up the regiment of being ready. It took a lot of effort to do that for the reality of what would have been for a portion of a season. All that effort and anxiety and hoping someone was going to screw up so I might get a chance," he added.

"Relief, disappointment, and sadness," he exclaimed. "I went through all of those things, from depression to being relieved that I don't have to go to work out as hard as I had to. I've been through a divorce, been through depression after finishing playing football, (and had) some heart issues where I've had procedures." Eddie describes his transition from professional football in two words. "Let down," he states. He is open to discuss his passion for the game and the inability to replace it. "To be honest, I don't think you ever will," he said. "It's not the same. Being in a high-level executive meeting is not like getting ready for the team dinner, going out for a football game, or as you're getting ready to go out for introductions before the game, running onto the field." Eddie misses his teammates and the camaraderie that came along with them. After losing both of his parents at such a young age he understands that the bond established with his teammates was probably greater as a result. "My family was football for a long period of time. I mean, I spent more time with teammates than I did my family, that's (the) reality," he said.

Currently, Eddie Murray is the director of Sports Medicine for a family-owned division of J and B Medical. He completes medical supply sale calls to the athletic trainers of high school, collegiate, and professional organizations. As emulated throughout his playing career, Eddie is a man of emotion and purpose, and has proven during his twenty-year NFL career that he is a survivor. He has the ability to change and adjust to adversity. These attributes, which he acquired as a professional athlete, will assist Eddie Murray as he continues to be an ambassador for his employer, as well as the game of football.

Chapter 5
JOE SCHMIDT

Joe Schmidt was selected All-Pro nine consecutive times during his thirteen-year tenure with the Detroit Lions. He was voted Lions MVP four times and NFL MVP in 1960. Joe played an important defensive role on the 1957 NFL Championship team. Following his playing career, he was named Lions head coach for seven seasons. Joe Schmidt was inducted into the NFL Hall of Fame in 1973.

As the youngest of four children, Joe Schmidt faced some of life's toughest lessons early on. He was raised by his mother in Pittsburgh, Pennsylvania following the death of his father and two older siblings. Joe channeled these tough times into a fiercely competitive attitude that was larger than his own physical stature. By the time he reached fifteen years of age he was already making his presence known in an adult football league coached by his oldest brother, John Schmidt. "Most of these guys were twenty-four-, twenty-five-, (and) twenty-six-year-olds," he said. "I was physically able to do it, and it was a good experience for me because I had to compete against older people and when you do that, you learn a lot and learn to compete," he added. "Every little town had teams and there was a lot of competition."

During his days at Brentwood High School not only did Joe excel at football but at basketball as well. "It was good for me from the standpoint of developing physical skills," he mentioned. "It teaches you quickness and defense and so forth, so it was a good addition to what I was doing in football." Following high school Joe received football offers from the University of Maryland, University of Cincinnati, and the University of Pittsburgh. "Being my father died when I was about twelve years old and my mother was by herself I elected to stay in Pittsburgh at the university," he stated. "I commuted back and forth to school."

As a second-string offensive fullback and first-string defensive linebacker, Joe found immediate success on defense, mostly because he naturally fell into the 4-3 defense that was evolving into the college game at the time. "All the time I was in high school I played middle linebacker so when the evolution came to the new defense it was easy for me because I had previously played it for a long time," he exclaimed. "A lot of guys who had never played that position were sort of struggling with it because of the fact that they were starting to throw the ball more and the whole middle was open so we had to do something about the guy in the middle, (and created) an even man line, and one thing led to another, and that's where I ended up," he added. As a middle linebacker Joe made All Big-East Conference as well as All-America before departing from the University of Pittsburgh.

Faced with a series of injuries that left him temporarily sidelined during his senior year of college Joe was tagged as injury prone leading into the NFL draft. Having played high school and college football in Pittsburgh, he was hoping to continue a professional football career with the local Pittsburgh Steelers. "I actually wanted to play for the Pittsburgh Steelers and they had indicated they were going to draft me," he stated. During the sixth round of the 1953 NFL draft, Pittsburgh attempted to pick Joe after selecting what they discovered was an ineligible player. Fortunately for the Detroit Lions, Pittsburgh quickly discovered that their pick was used with that initial choice. "So the next round, which was the seventh round, the Detroit Lions drafted me," he said. "At that particular time I was very disappointed because I wanted to stay in Pittsburgh and stay closer to home. So I was drafted by the Lions who were champions that year and I didn't figure I had a chance to make the team, but everything turned out for the best," he added.

Despite his concern of simply making the team, Joe became one of the best players in the NFL during his thirteen seasons in Detroit. From the opening day he was a starting linebacker and would call the team's defensive signals as captain by mid-season. Joe's fierce, competitive style helped secure a NFL Championship in 1957. It also got him selected for nine consecutive Pro-Bowls, four Lion MVP's, and a NFL MVP award in 1960. Joe Schmidt became one of the best middle linebackers in the history of the game and the standard by which all others were judged. He remained humble throughout the countless accolades and continued to give credit to his teammates. "We had a great football team and a great defensive line," he exclaimed. "Which, incidentally, anybody who has a good middle linebacker has a great defensive line. I'm not trying to be humble about this, it's just a fact that we did have defensive football players that were exceptionally good (including) Alex Karras, Sam Williams, and Roger Brown," he added. Joe also remained humble when he turned in his Lions jersey for an Army Reserve uniform in order to serve his country for six months' active duty shortly after winning the 1957 NFL championship.

In addition to his football career, Joe pursued other interests, as well. "I was in the restaurant business with a guy and he had a restaurant on the east side," he shared. "The Golden Lion in Grosse Pointe." Joe's partner would not need to worry about him eating the profits as the Detroit Lions assisted in this matter. "We would get weighed every Friday and you had to meet a particular assigned weight otherwise they would fine you," he humorously said.

Toward the last few years of his professional football career Joe found himself facing some serious injuries. The time away from playing while injured allowed him to contemplate his professional future and forced him to think about other opportunities years before he actually finished. "I had two severely dislocated shoulders, both had required surgery," he stated. "And for that reason I said, *You'd better start thinking about what you're going to do after this thing.* So I went to work for this gentleman who had a gear and tool company and he said, 'You can go around and start making calls for me,' so I did that," he said. "I did that for one off-season and then I met some people who were in the manufacturing agency business and I picked up another line from another guy. The year after that I met a gentleman who had a rubber line (and) we got to know each other pretty well, so we started a company together," he added. "His name was Smith and mine was Schmidt, so we called (the company) Smith and Schmidt. It's boring, but that's what it was," he joked. "I worked during the off-season and (during the season) every Monday. We had Mondays off, so I would go to the office and then work a half-day on Tuesdays after practice. I'd go to the office and make some calls and do some things. The automotive business was much different than it is today, there wasn't as much competition," he exclaimed. "At that time, you know, Ted

Lindsay was around doing this and guys from baseball. (Athletes) that would stay here in Detroit had an opportunity. In other towns, I used to talk to some of the other ball players and they would say, 'Boy, you're fortunate to be working in Detroit and playing for the Detroit Lions because these other teams don't have the industrial base that Detroit has.' It's a very prosperous town that loves their athletes and loves their teams, so the result is it helps you quite a bit. It opens doors," he said.

It was a combination of foresight gained during injuries, hard work, and the benefit of being based in Detroit that prevented Joe's transition out of professional football from being too abrupt financially. "I made more money in the off-season than I did playing," he boasted. "I could have probably played (longer), but I figured it's time I think about (retiring). If I didn't have the surgeries I don't think I would have quit, but I had two very difficult surgeries on my shoulders and a lot of rehabilitation. I didn't want to go again," he added. "If I would dislocate them I would need more surgery, plus the fact that we didn't have a very good football team. If we had a better football team I would have taken the chance, but that wasn't the case. As a result, I just felt I should leave," he said.

From a practical perspective, the transition from professional football back to normal, everyday life didn't take long. "Thirty minutes," Joe laughed. During this era of professional football it was common for the athletes to work in addition to playing. Another reason why Joe's transition from professional football may have been so easy at this time was because it didn't last very long. He came back, not as a player but this time as a coach. One year after his retirement Joe was asked to be an assistant coach for the Lions and by the following year was given the reins as the Lions' head coach. "I wasn't prepared and I'll be the first one to say anything," he said. "I wasn't prepared to be a coach. And to tell you the honest truth, I don't think it was the right thing to do, but it was offered to me and I knew in my heart what had to be done to be a successful football team. I thought if I did that we could be halfway successful," he added. "I knew the guys on the team because I had played with them for a few years."

As a coach, applying a winning mentality to his team came easy as Joe simply used the same mindset he had as a player, which was conducive to winning and preparing to win. "Don't beat yourself," he'd preach. "It's hard enough to win when the other team beats you." What didn't come easy was the challenge that arose from coaching many of his old teammates, so soon after he had played. "It was difficult for me and they watched me very closely," he stated. "I could feel their eyes on me analyzing everything I did, and it was very stressful. The first two years weren't rosy, but we became a pretty good football team." One of the reasons for the improvement was defensive back Lem Barney, who "was like an angel falling out of the sky," according to Joe. The two would spend seven years together, working to improve the club and have a good time while doing so. "You have to have a good time at what you're doing; otherwise, you're not going to like it," he stated. "I think you can make a jump and still compete and be a tough and well-coached football team and still have a good time." Following his seventh season of coaching Joe decided it was time to get out of football and focus on his business again.

Being able to transition from player to coach before leaving the NFL assisted his transition from professional football. "I think it helped," he said. "It was a good experience. I grew from the experience, it taught me a lot about life, about myself, about human beings, and so forth." It also taught Joe more about leadership and a different way to handle adversity. "As a player you take disappointment in a different way, you take it individually," he explained. "When you coach, you take it overall as you're the one responsible for the disappointment. You're the one responsible for the loss." Joe applied other attributes that were gained from professional football. "If you had enough aggressiveness with you, you (could) prove that you could do the job, and you were accountable, and were there in the event that they needed some help," he said. "I think that's the number one thing when you're an athlete, people are thinking that you're going to walk in and give you an order, but it's just the opposite. They want you to prove even over and above the ordinary guy that walks in. Everybody doesn't accept you with open arms, I mean, there were people who didn't like athletes necessarily," he added. "It wasn't (like) here's a guy that plays for the Detroit Lions, walk in, and I'll give you some business. You have to override all of those things and sometimes it gets to the point where it's a little annoying, and if you're not tenacious enough about it and you don't have a real passion for success, then you're not going to accomplish much. You're not going to last," he exclaimed.

Joe worked hard to shake the image associated with being a former professional athlete. He did his homework and became more confident in his knowledge and understanding of his business while gaining motivation from his cynics. "It's the same things you have in athletics that you can apply to the business world," he said. "(It's) just a matter of preparation and desire to be successful. When someone tells you (athletes) can't do it because you don't know what you're talking about or you don't have the background; that ignites my motivation. So I'm going to prove you wrong," he added.

Joe ultimately experienced much financial success in his business, but still found a void from the absence of football. "The emotional side is probably the biggest thing," he stated. "It's the loss of not having a group of guys and support around you. All of a sudden, *boom*, they're gone, everybody is going in different ways and you're by yourself," he added. Joe discovered that passion was the largest missing emotion. "That's the bad thing. It's one of the things that you have difficulty in replacing in your life," he exclaimed. "I haven't found anything that really comes close. Every day you have to get up ready for practice, you have to excel at practice, you have to be prepared. You're building every week for this big crescendo that's going to be on Sunday," he added. "Win or lose, it's exciting, and it stimulates you and brings you to something where you're being tried all of the time and I sort of like that. I miss the opportunity to be with a group of guys who have the same passion we're talking about, to reach a certain goal. To be willing to put your inequities aside in order to accomplish that, whatever their outside enjoyment is, they do everything they possibly can as a group to be successful," he said. "Business doesn't work that way because people don't have the mentality an athlete has, and they try to take that philosophy and bring it into the work force, but it's difficult to get them all," he added. "If you can take that psychological aspect and carry it over into the so-called real world, then you can stand out because a lot of people don't have that desire. I used to try that mentality, and got it to the point where, you know, we're in this together, do you want to make money or you here to just have a good time. I mean, that's our number one thing, number one passion, if you want money, work hard, get the orders, you get money. You don't have to write a book about it, to me it's a very cut and dry thing." Something Joe didn't find cut and dry was the lack of feedback he was accustomed to as an athlete. "In sports I had feedback all of the time," he said. "I knew exactly where I stood, I'm either good or bad or I did this or I did a bad play. When you're (on the sidelines) you know exactly what you have to do to get back on the field by next Sunday. When you step into the football field everybody can see what the hell you're doing. It's like looking in your office every day, people have an opportunity to invade your privacy to look in and see how you're doing," he added. "I don't know anyplace in life where people have an opportunity, like in athletics, to make an analysis on their own to what good you are and what good you've done for the team. I mean, I can't go up to an office in General Motors or the President and watch those guys. We answered every Sunday, right after the game. Nobody in the world has that stigma, that burden of being able to tell why we were successful or why we were not successful immediately after it happens," he stated. "Sometimes in business you don't have the luxury of knowing where you are and it comes to a point where you're like, am I in this thing or am I not in it. Until I get the job and somebody gives me a piece of paper that I have a job, I don't know," he said. "I guess the real reason why we don't have a stigma, so to speak, is nobody knows what the hell you're doing. You simply walk around in a suit, dressed up. You're working on things and get a paycheck in ten or twelve months," he added.

Joe now uses football analogies to express his philosophy of life. "On the football field you start here and you got to get there, and you say, how am I going to get from here to there," he exclaimed. "There's certain rules and regulations you have to follow in order to get there. You have a goal every time you step on it. (This is) one of the many analogies in football to life."

Presently in the golden years of his life, Joe counts his blessings and acknowledges the many successes he experienced beyond the football field. "I've been successful in business and I've been able to make a good living for my family with enough funds to live relatively nice in my old age," he said. "My family is fine, kids are good, so I thank the good Lord," he added. "I've been very fortunate in my life. The transition might be at times, not what I exactly wanted, but you get through life with a clean slate. I've been around a lot of nice people, good people, good to me in business and sports and I cannot complain one bit about what happened to me when I came here to Detroit," he stated. "I've been through some major problems health-wise; prostrate cancer, open heart surgery, cataracts, (but) I've been fortunate health-wise to survive those things. I thank the dear Lord every night that I had another day. I've been married over forty-six years, today that's a miracle. I was very fortunate to marry a girl who understood, I'd be lost without her," he exclaimed. Marilynn and Joe have raised five children together and claim that they have never caused them one bit of trouble. "Good Christian kids," he stated. "Until they put me in the grave, I think that I've been far and above fortunate." Let's hope that Joe Schmidt can continue to feel fortunate for many more years.

Chapter 6
HARVEY MARLATT

The Detroit Pistons drafted Harvey Marlatt the same year as Bob Lanier. Chosen in the sixteenth round, Marlatt would play with Hall of Fame teammates Dave Bing and Lanier during his three-year NBA tenure. Though brief, his professional career remained impacting as it was against legends such as Jerry West, Oscar Robinson, and Wilt Chamberlin—to name a few.

Harvey Marlatt began to athletically blossom at the beginning of high school when he moved from Atlanta, Michigan, to the neighboring community of Alpena. Excelling mostly in football and basketball at Alpena High School, he received All State honors in both sports and All-America Honorable Mention status in basketball. Part of Harvey's development and success could be attributed to Bill Frieder, who was his junior varsity basketball coach at Alpena High. Frieder eventually became the head basketball coach at the University of Michigan. Little did Harvey know that he would encounter another Big Ten coaching connection in the likes of Jim Dutcher, who was coaching basketball at Alpena Community College when he was in high school. Harvey signed a letter of intent to play basketball at

Alpena Community College but followed Dutcher to his new position as head coach at Eastern Michigan University (EMU). Harvey completed his four years at Eastern and Dutcher ultimately moved on to coach at the University of Minnesota.

EMU was experiencing a tremendous amount of growth at this time, raising their enrollment from 8,000 to 17,000 students by the time Harvey graduated. As an independent college that wasn't affiliated with an athletic conference at this time he had a unique experience and stated, "The schedule was like you'd be playing Hillsdale (College) one day and playing DePaul (University) or somebody the next. You know, Marquette (University) or somebody, so it was really kind of a weird deal. They (Eastern) were trying to go big time and everything. They were really putting on the growth, so our schedule was pretty well reflected in that," he added. Over his four years at Eastern it became apparent that the school wasn't the only thing heading for the big time. Harvey was voted team captain during his junior and senior seasons and earned second team All-America honors as a senior.

Taking pleasure in the game of basketball, Harvey didn't give much thought to playing after college. "I really just enjoyed the game at the time," he said. "I really didn't think about (going pro) a whole lot, I don't know why." It wasn't until he was contacted by the New York Nets of the American Basketball Association (ABA) that the realization of this possibility even occurred for him. Based on a recommendation by former Marquette University coach Al McGuire, the Nets eventually drafted Harvey in the fifth round. In 1970 another draft was in the works with the National Basketball Association (NBA). The Detroit Pistons would pick Harvey in the sixteenth round. He would attend the Nets camp first, but did not make the team. "(I was) the thirteenth man on a twelve-man roster," he joked. Harvey decided to attend the Pistons training camp, which ironically was being held at his alma mater, Eastern Michigan University. An event that happened during the three-week training camp would make or break the chances of Harvey making the team. This event occurred between number one Piston draft pick Bob Lanier and Harvey, who was the drafted 224th. "I went after a loose ball and hit (Lanier) right across the knee," he stated. "It popped, and I was like, oh boy, I'm out of here, they're going to get rid of me now. But it turned out all I did was break some adhesions in (his) knee and actually made it better. So it turned out okay and they didn't usher me out of the gym or get rid of me," he exclaimed.

Harvey's professional basketball experience was a balance between the exhilaration of making the team and being awestruck. "When you're watching guys like (Wilt) Chamberlin and Jerry West and Oscar Robinson when you're in high school and then all of a sudden you're there," he said. "The first year was, you know, it was kind of an eye opener. I remember in a shoot around when someone introduced me to Wilt and honest to God, this guy's arms were as big as my leg. The most intimidating person I've ever seen in my life," he added. Harvey's observation was reinforced when he ran into a pick from Chamberlin and stated, "I might as well run right into a wall. It was like everything crumbled."

Harvey's humble upbringing was a far cry from the city lights and glitz of the NBA. "I wasn't very street-wise when I first got there," he stated. "Coming from a little farm in northern Michigan to all of a sudden playing in Madison Square Garden or the LA Forum, I kind of got wise fairly quick."

Now, playing against the players he once idolized, Harvey recalls a comment that was made to him in high school. "We played Highland Park at Cobo Arena in a preliminary game before the Lakers and Pistons game when I was in high school," he said. "I can remember that a guy who really meant a lot to me, Jerry West, made a comment about me playing in the preliminary game and that I was a nice player. He was my idol at the time so that really meant a lot," he shared. "Then you get to guard him later on."

Harvey was a marginal NBA player and didn't get much playing time. "(I was) one of those borderline guys, just on the bench," he stated. But as a result of an eye injury to teammate Dave Bing, he was given more playing time in his third season. As Harvey experienced three head coaches in three years, he began to experience a breakup of his Pistons team. "It kind of fell apart," he said. "It was actually kind of frustrating and, you know, I was still at that point wanting to play because of the game and all," he added. "I didn't understand the business part of it and nobody was there to tell me anything about it. You never know, there's no guarantee or certainty if you're going to be there the next day."

Harvey admitted he didn't understand the business part of the game, but was forced to do so when he was released at the end of his third year, the day before he would've qualified for an NBA pension. "That's when the business part hit me," he said. "I would have qualified for a pension, so that was a little bitterness. I got let go one day short of getting a pension." These bitter feelings influenced his next decision and changed the course of the rest of his life. He was asked by the Pistons to go to Grand Rapids and play for a semi-professional team, but at this point was emotionally all but checked out of basketball. "I guess I kind of just had a negative reaction, a little bitterness because of the time I got released," he stated. "I just turned them down." In addition to this opportunity Harvey turned down a chance to play for an ABA team in Memphis.

You'd think that a professional athlete would do anything to sustain his playing career, but in this case, Harvey's resentment rang stronger than his desire to play, and he later regretted it. "I actually, which was dumb, went back up north," he said. "(Memphis) was trying to get a hold of me and I just decided that, you know, all that pressure, and I had a son just born, and I'm going to finish school. That probably wasn't a very good choice." His regret was reinforced when he learned that the ABA and NBA merged not long thereafter. "I think one thing that was agonizing to me was that I really didn't go back and give it another shot," he shared.

Refocused on completing a partial semester of college and student teaching, Harvey was excited to discover a teaching job in his old hometown of Atlanta, Michigan. "I was always big in the outdoors stuff," he said. "The hunting and fishing, that's why I always wanted to get back up here, you know, because I can be in my deer blind in five minutes or a trout stream in fifteen. Those type of things, which really was stuff that I had done at a very young age and I still do today."

Harvey jumped on the opportunity to become a varsity basketball coach at Atlanta High School after a couple of years of teaching and coaching junior high baseball and basketball. There was a huge pay cut from his NBA league minimum salary of $18,000 to the $7,000 he would make his first year of teaching. His transition from professional basketball became a matter of sublimating an outlet. Harvey took the energy that he used while playing professional basketball and directed it into teaching, coaching, being a driver education instructing, hunting, and fishing. "I don't know if I replaced (playing basketball)," he said. "But it was an outlet for me, I enjoyed that and so it was an easy transition as far as finding something to do, occupy my time, and I enjoyed it. I really kept myself busy," he added. In addition to finding new outlets Harvey attributes his easy transition to the reality of his NBA status. "I think (my transition) was low key because I never was real high in the NBA position anyway so I didn't have far to drop, let's say, or as far to come down," he said. "I don't think anything probably can replace your competitiveness in the game itself. You know, when you're competing at a high level or even at a lesser level, the competition is what attracts you," he added. "I always felt that I never played or coached a game that I couldn't win. I've told my players that and I've always felt that. We might be big underdogs but I always felt we were going to win."

It's clear that Harvey has transitioned from competing as a player to competing as a coach and more. "You can still be competitive," he said. "In other words, if I'm building a work bench, I want to build it really good. If I'm fishing, I want to do it right. If I'm hunting, I want to do it right. For example, I don't shoot the first little deer that steps into the woods in front of me, or catch all of the little fish out of the stream," he added. "You may fish for that one big one you know is there but haven't caught."

Some of Harvey's successes since leaving professional basketball can be paralleled to some of life's simple pleasures, but to him they mean just as much. Being around as his children grew and now his grandchildren he considers an important indulgence. Clearly Harvey lists his family as his biggest success, with coaching not far behind. He takes great pride in the fact that his players have posted a decent showing during his tenure as the varsity basketball coach at Atlanta High School. Also, he's become some type of northern Michigan land baron as he's combined the family farms and purchased more adjacent property over the years. Harvey's property now equals a combined 600 acres of land and includes an area deemed Marlatt Mountain, on top of where he built a cabin on stilts. "Heck of a view," he said.

Harvey expressed great pride in his induction into the Eastern Michigan University Hall of Fame, which occurred when he was twenty-five years old. He spoke of the induction ceremony with humor as well as pride. "I thought it was for old people and I still had long hair," he said. "The funny story is that I was so worried that the old people (being inducted) were going to fall off the stage and the first thing I know I slid my chair and went right off the back," he laughed. Harvey was also inducted into the Alpena High School Hall of Fame at a young age and wondered if there was more to it. "I thought maybe it was a bad omen that I was going to pass away or something," he stated.

Harvey has come full circle from whence he came and was quite comfortable with that path. He thrives on the things that we often take for granted or are too busy to acknowledge. To be able to experience the thrill of fierce competition at a professional level and yet be delighted with the great outdoors or the presence of a grandchild exemplifies Harvey Marlatt. In his own simple way he has impacted countless people around him, which is probably more than he'll ever know. The multitude of students he's taught, the players he's coached, and perhaps the others who have simply heard about this former NBA player who now lives in their tiny community. Naming the area where Harvey's home was built on his 600-acre spread "Marlatt Mountain" is to a certain extent symbolic of the life he has led; solid, grand, yet simple.

Chapter 7
GREG KELSER

Greg Kelser was Academic and Athletic All-America at Michigan State University. Together with legendary teammate Earvin "Magic" Johnson he won a NCAA National Championship in 1979 against basketball legend, Larry Bird and Indiana State University. Following his first-round draft by the Detroit Pistons, Greg played in the NBA for six seasons before experiencing a chronic career ending injury.

Greg Kelser knew early on in his athletic career that basketball was going to be his ticket. He used the other sports at Detroit Henry Ford High School to enhance his quickness and stay in shape for basketball. "I was growing," he stated. "Loved football, very good at baseball, but those are two sports that I didn't have the necessary size to continue playing. I was very skinny. Basketball was the one sport that I was able to keep up with the competition, so that became the sport of choice," he added.

With All-City and All-State basketball honors by the time he left high school, Greg set off to find a college. His serious considerations were Arizona State University, University of Minnesota, Central Michigan University, University of Michigan, and Michigan State University. "I took my first official visit to the University of Minnesota and had a great time," he stated. "They were high on my list and I also had a great time visiting Arizona State University. They had a very good basketball team. I wasn't really worried too much about academics because I knew wherever I go, if I applied myself I would get a good education," he added. "For me Michigan State served just a tremendous purpose because it allowed me to be away from home yet be close enough to home so I could get there if I needed to, and it also (gave) my parents the opportunity to attend all my games over the four-year span, every single game. And that was something I would not have had if I had gone to Minnesota or something, I would have not had if I gone to Arizona State so Michigan State in that regard was perfect," he exclaimed. "Plus, it offered a great opportunity to play right away, which I did."

Greg experienced two major accomplishments during his tenure at MSU, which included winning the NCAA National Championship in 1979 with teammate Earvin "Magic" Johnson against Larry Bird and Indiana State University. "Clearly the biggest athletic feat," he stated. "That was a dream come true for all of my coaches and teammates. (It) was something we set out to do in the beginning of the year. Without question it was the most terrific highlight that I had at Michigan State."

The second major collegiate accomplishment for Greg didn't occur on the basketball court but in the classroom as he was selected Academic All-America his senior year. "Being named to the Academic All-America team was really a highlight because it showed a lot of people that I had balance," he said. "I was an All-American in the classroom, I was an All-American on the court, how much more balanced can you get than that? I am very proud of it," he added. Though proud of this accomplishment, Greg gives much credit to his parents. "If it wouldn't have been for them pushing that would have never happened," he admits. "I probably would have just been content staying eligible, they were the ones who pushed me."

Greg felt fortunate and very fulfilled by the honors he received at MSU. "I got everything that I was supposed to get," he stated. "I got an education, I (eventually) got my degree, and I excelled at sports. So much so that it allowed me the opportunity to be drafted in the first round of the NBA draft in 1979. I couldn't have asked for more," he added.

Greg became a Detroit Piston when he was drafted three picks behind the NBA's number one overall pick and MSU teammate, Earvin "Magic" Johnson. "I think I knew after my junior year that I would be a first round draft pick," he said. "It was just a matter of how high. Obviously, by the time we made it to the tournament I then thought I would possibly be a top ten pick. By winning the NCAA championship and having that stage to demonstrate my talent, I felt pretty safe and secure that I would be a top five pick," he added. "Being drafted was an absolute thrill!"

Now playing amongst the top basketball players in the world, Greg still remained true to his athletic and academic focus as he spent the first two off-seasons in the NBA finishing up his degree. "During my days at MSU I never went to summer school," he said. "Once I finished my four years, I still needed twenty-six more credits. After my first year in the NBA I went back to school and got the first thirteen of those remaining twenty-six. And after the second year I got the second thirteen and graduated," he boasted. Greg obtained his degree in Social Science and Criminal Justice, and admitted that there were a couple of underlying people who motivated his academic completion. "My parents were clearly on me to get it finished, but so was Jud Heathcote," he said. "He constantly called me to say, 'Hey, when are you going to do it?' He wanted to make sure I didn't let it slide and that I didn't wait until my NBA career was over. As (Jud) said, they would talk to recruits and parents about my success in the classroom, but they couldn't tell people what my degree was in because I didn't have one. It was important to finish the deal," he added.

Greg's first two seasons in the NBA were personally solid but a far cry from the team success he previously experienced as a NCAA champion. He averaged fourteen points per game as an NBA rookie, but the Pistons had a 16-66 and 21-61 respective win-loss record in those two seasons. "As far as highlights are concerned, I didn't have many with the Pistons," he explained. "We were not a very good team my two years, the two full years with the Pistons, we weren't very good, we were young," he admitted. "But you know, the thrill of competing, being out there competing, and then getting out there and being able to play against a lot of the greats that I grew up watching, that was just incredible. And seeing how different the game is from the college game. Having to bring it every night (mentally and physically) was a true transition. Not being able to take any nights off, otherwise, you wind up getting embarrassed and that was never something you wanted to have happen," he added.

Winning ways would once again return to Greg, but it came in the form of a mid-season trade to the Seattle Supersonics. "I got my first taste of the playoffs," he said. "We were a very good team in Seattle, a team that was good enough to challenge for a championship, at least a championship contender. Unfortunately for us at the time, we were playing against famous teams like the Lakers and they were making it to the finals practically every year. No matter how good we were, we could just never get away from them. You know, Earvin and Kareem, Norm Nixon, and James Worthy, and Jamaal Wilkes and all of the rest. They were just one of the best teams of all times," he exclaimed.

Following a two-season stint with the Sonics, Greg found himself playing for the Clippers, who were in San Diego at this time. His NBA career became a short road soon after this move, mostly because of chronic injuries and the lack of a legitimate contract offer. "My knee problems started my second year in," he stated. "From year two to the sixth I was never 100%. That's not an excuse, that's something that probably 50% of the players who play can say," he exclaimed. "Basketball is a very demanding sport on the body for a guy like myself who is not the biggest person in the world and really depends on quickness and speed. When I started to have knee problems my ability was somewhat compromised. I found myself needing anti-inflammatories to control the pain and swelling in my knees (in order) to really get out there and perform, and that is never a good thing," he admitted. "When by the end of my fifth season, if I had gotten a legitimate contract offer I would have continued playing, and would have continued to do what I needed to do to stay on the floor. I did not get a fair offer and I ended up being a free agent that year and holding out like a lot of free agents did, and like a lot of free agents, we didn't get signed. So later in that year I ended up finishing with the Indiana Pacers," he said. "That was my sixth season in the league and when that was over I was at pretty much the same situation, waiting for a contract offer, a good contract offer, a fair contract offer, and one did not come. That is when I started looking at other avenues. I had the opportunity to go overseas, but I wasn't enthused about that, I wanted to be an NBA player. That wasn't going to be the case (so) I made the decision to start looking at my next career," he added. "I was still able to play six seasons and I feel very blessed to have had that. I would have loved for my career to have lasted more years, that would have been just incredible, but it didn't, it lasted six years, which is six years longer than most," he boasted. "With all of that, I didn't win a championship, I didn't get to experience the pinnacle like I did in college, but I played with some really good teams. I played basketball with some of the greatest players ever to lace up a pair of shoes. I was there working hard against them every day and for me, I feel very blessed to have been able to have that opportunity."

Fortunately, Greg possessed a foresight that motivated him to prepare for the next phase of his life before his final NBA season. He credits this insightful knowledge to his mother and father. "I had parents who used to always stress that that day would come," he said. "They used that to motivate me educationally and it was them who reminded me that even when I was playing and having success as a pro, I needed to think about life after basketball. I don't know where I would be without them," he stated. "I started to prepare myself as early as the third year in the league. A very good friend by the name of Charlie Neal, who is like a brother to me, was a local sportscaster at Channel 2 in Detroit. He eventually became a sports director at Black Entertainment Television. I spent a lot of time with him at the station and just hanging out and getting somewhat familiar with broadcasting and the various nuances of commentating. I decided that that was something I might look into once my career was over. Bob Page had a great impact, as well. The two of them were probably the biggest reason why I was able to get the opportunity in broadcasting that I got," he stated.

Following the 1984–1985 NBA season, Greg took some time off to hone his broadcasting skills. "I took the whole season off," he explained. "I was working on trying to be the very best that I could be so when the opportunity came, I'd be ready. I wanted to make sure I was competent; I wanted to make sure everything was in place. When that time came in 1986 I decided okay, I'm ready to go, and Charlie was able to give me some opportunities," he said. "I was able to fall into some broadcasting at college as well as later on working with the Pistons. That was my springboard, so to speak. The time that he spent with me, the mentoring that he provided, I owe him a lot," he added.

Now, twenty-plus years into the broadcasting business, Greg still recalls the difficulties that ensued after his final professional playing days. "When I got into broadcasting I was not thirty yet, I was probably twenty-nine years old," he said. "I still had a strong passion for playing the game. I missed the competition, first and foremost. It was difficult sometimes, especially at the pro level. When I would broadcast games for the Pistons I can't tell you how difficult it was sometimes to sit there and watch and not have that urge, overwhelming sometimes," he admitted. "It was a precedent to do my job, but you know, I (found) myself in the gym the next morning working out, trying to release that pent-up energy. I would say that was probably about the first six or seven years of my broadcasting career," he added. "When you leave the game at twenty-eight, I had been playing up to that point, eighteen or nineteen straight years of organized basketball; when October comes around, you are getting ready for camp, you are getting ready for the team, you are getting ready for the practice, all of that stuff. Just walking away from something that had become such a part of me, from fifth grade through middle school, and then high school, then college, and then the NBA, it just seemed like a natural thing to do, play basketball. You could almost center your watch (and) calendar by it," he exclaimed. "The most difficult thing was giving that up, having to accept the fact that you are not doing that anymore.

Come October you got to do something else, you don't have a team to get ready for. That was difficult," he said. "When that goes it's a void. There's a void there. And I don't care how successful your career has been, I don't care how much money you have been able to stash away, there is still a void. And none of that can be replaced," he added.

Though unable to replace this void, Greg at least found something that assisted in fulfilling his competitive edge. "I continued to play a lot of AAU basketball, travel basketball, where I found competition," he stated. "Not like the NBA, but it was against a lot of former NBA players. I was able to do that until I was about thirty-five-thirty-six years old. Not having to go at it every day like you have in the NBA (allowed me) to do it without a lot of pain that I was given with when I left the NBA," he exclaimed. "I could pull away when I needed to, and you don't get that option when you play professionally, it's your job. We won the AAU championship three years in a row down in Topeka, Kansas. By the time I was thirty-six, I pretty much exercised all that was still there, I could finally sit down and broadcast a game without feeling like I got to get out there. Around that time I picked up the game of golf, and that provided a new challenge, one that I still pursue," he added.

Over time and with the implementation of other sublimating activities, Greg was able to be more comfortable with his transition from playing basketball. He eventually got to the point where he was able to move on and totally let his athletic past go. "I don't miss anything now," he stated. "Because, you know, I can't play anymore. I think once you get to a point where you can truly look yourself in the mirror and say, 'I can't do it anymore,' you are better off. I couldn't honestly look in the mirror probably the first five, six years once I retired, I felt like I could still (play). I know I can't (play) now! I don't miss anything now about playing, nothing at all. It's gone, out of my system," he claims.

Greg has transcended his focus and drive into his next career—broadcasting. "My passion now is just working as a broadcaster and to be as good as I possibly can," he said. "And I love it when people come up to me. Just last night I had a guy come up to me, thanking me, and he said, 'I love the way you broadcast and my wife loves the way you broadcast because you really explain the game and simplify it for her.' I loved that! That's the key for me, that's my challenge now. To compete and do that and then try to improve," he stated.

With only limited spots available in TV broadcasting Greg understands that he must continue to work hard in order to maintain his status as a broadcaster. "There is a lot of competition for those limited spots, so you'd better keep working and you had better be trying to get better," he stated. "I am very fortunate and blessed to be able to do it."

Currently, Greg continues to improve himself and not rest on his past successes. He's seen the progress he's made from broadcasting the boys and girls high school playoffs, to the NCAA men's and women's tournament, to the WNBA and NBA finals, and settles for nothing short of excellence. Like in college, when he earned both academic and athletic All-America honors, Greg drives himself in more than one aspect of his life. "I do a lot of other stuff," he stated. "I run basketball camps, do a lot of public speaking, I volunteer. I have a beautiful wife that I have been married to for twenty years," he added.

When referring to life's opportunities, Greg provides some very sound advice. "Cherish it," he exclaims. "Do your best to get the very most out of it." Based on the continued accomplishments Greg Kelser has accumulated since his final professional playing days, it is safe to say that he continues to live his own advice.

Chapter 8
KELLY TRIPUCKA

Kelly Tripucka was named one of the top 100 All-time High School Athletes in New Jersey. He was voted to the collegiate All-America list three times before departing from the University of Notre Dame. Kelly averaged more than seventeen points per game over the course of his ten-year NBA career.

You might think that the solid sports tradition of Kelly Tripucka's family would make his athletic life a walk in the park. With a father who played in the NFL and older brothers who laid a foundation in college athletics, much was established before him. Despite these facts, Kelly did not rest on the family's athletic laurels. In fact, rather than accepting any walk in a park, he was often found running, since a young age, on the basketball courts of Bloomfield's Brookside Park during many New Jersey summer nights. It was while playing with his four brothers under the lights that Kelly learned the true meaning of competition. No one wanted to lose and then sit a multitude of games before regaining the court. Kelly learned that his family's previous successes did not matter, and they actually inspired him to work harder and achieve even more.

Not only did Kelly work to achieve in basketball but other sports as well. He can partially credit his father's wisdom as the reason for his involvement. "It used to be a rule at our house that my father said, 'Don't come home because you are not going to sit around doing nothing, so go find something else to do,'" he stated. Kelly followed his father's advice while attending Bloomfield High School and participated on the school's soccer team, for which he was named All-State and eventually won a state championship. He also high jumped and threw both the discus and javelin, for which he won a state title while being considered one of the best in the country. Kelly attributes many of his high school accomplishments to his coaches. "I had great coaching," he exclaims. "They had a lot to do with my success. I had a soccer coach that had been coaching Bloomfield High soccer for over thirty years; I had a track guy that had been there thirty years. We had a legendary (basketball) coach named George Cella, and he had won over 500 games. He was kind of like the John Wooden of his time. As a kid growing up, the big thing was going to go play for Coach Cella and having the opportunity to do so, and watching four older brothers play for him and see the championships that he won and all of the things that he did, and how everybody respected him," he added. "He had that kind of special aura about him."

Despite having much success in other sports, Kelly knew basketball would be his passion. "I was born and known for my basketball," he said. "Even though I enjoyed playing three sports and the competition and going from season to season, I still knew that I would probably have my most success and chance to advance further on to college and have an opportunity to get a scholarship somewhere playing basketball. I played those (other) sports because of the competition, to be better than somebody else, or to better myself," he added. "To set records or to be part of a team. My brothers had done a couple of those things, so I figured, that looks like fun. Let's try it."

By his senior year in high school, Kelly made it clear that basketball was his number one passion by scoring over 1,000 points his final year and accumulating close to 2,300 points total. This was especially amazing considering the shorter amount of time he had to do it. "We had a three-year high school," he said. "(I) didn't play as a freshman because I was in junior high. I think I really blossomed my junior year. I scored about thirty points a game and that's when I knew people were interested in me, and that I had a really good shot of going someplace and getting a scholarship, playing in a big-time program."

Kelly acknowledges and credits his family for the college groundwork laid before him. "I am so lucky in that regard because all my brothers went on to play either college football or college basketball," he shared. "They were all scholarship athletes. Chris went to Boston College and played football. T.K., he is the biggest of the lot because he is like six foot nine (and) played basketball at Florida University and New York. Todd played at Lafayette College in Eastern Pennsylvania. Mark played (quarterback) at the University of Massachusetts. I never looked at that as a pressure point, but I think it was more of living up to the expectations of what the brothers had set," he added. "I pretty much had my pick of where I wanted to go, but I had an idea early on. I narrowed it down to four schools."

Duke University, University of Notre Dame, University of Maryland, and University of South Carolina all had a good shot at landing this stellar athlete out of New Jersey, but Kelly clearly made up his mind. "People say I went to Notre Dame because of my father," he said. "My father never put any pressure on me.

Notre Dame was just right at the time. The way the basketball program was coming around, they were starting to get a name for themselves, and obviously, you can't beat the reputation or the education. It was just right," he added. When confronted by then Maryland coach Lefty Driesell, about the reason for choosing Notre Dame, Kelly initially fumbled, but then gave his answer. "I thought about it for a second and said it's because Notre Dame wasn't part of a conference. It had been independent," he said. "They played all over the country. They went to the East Coast, they went down south, they went up north, went out west. You name it (they) played anybody, anytime, anywhere. I told him that had a lot to do with it, and without missing a beat, Mr. Driesell tells me in his southern twang, 'Oh hell, Kelly, if you'd told me that yesterday, we would have quit the ACC.' He was a heck of a nice guy," he added.

As a young collegian at Notre Dame, Kelly experienced immediate athletic success. "We went to the Final Four my freshman year," he stated. "You're less than a year removed from playing high school basketball and the next thing you know, you're playing in the Final Four. I wasn't intimidated by anybody," he said. "(I) was named Midwest Regional MVP that year to get us to the Final Four." Unfortunately, Kelly's team would not make it there again. "The Final Four experience, it came so quick," he said. "I don't think I enjoyed it or took the time to enjoy it that much. You probably figure you'll get back there so it won't matter. We never got back there. We got close a couple of times," he added.

Although, his team did not make another appearance in an NCAA Final Four, Kelly left his mark. "I ended up being a three-time All-American," he said. "We won some big-time games. We beat, I think, five or six #1-ranked teams during the course of (my) four years," he added. Despite the many personal and team accomplishments at Notre Dame, Kelly did not think about the NBA. "I never even thought it about," he admits. "The pros, I mean it's the pros. At the time Kareem Abdul-Jabbar, Dr. J, Larry Bird, (and) Magic Johnson were there. Even though he was my age, you just kind of never... I watched pros and I'm like I'm not good enough to play against those guys. Not that I was afraid of them, but you know, they're the pros," he added. "I ended up getting drafted and still worried about getting cut. I mean, maybe that was naïve or whatever. I think it was such a big time and such a pinnacle of success, I wouldn't say there was doubt, but you just almost didn't believe you were there. That it was happening." Kelly clarified his feelings more. "I knew that when you're in high school, you were a big fish in a little pond," he said. "College, you're a big fish in a big pond. I knew there was going to be better players, better competition, but I was willing to make that extra effort and sacrifice to be better. I just thought, *I'm ready for this.* I won't say that I wasn't ready for the pros, because as it turned out I was. I just never allowed myself to feel comfortable. I never allowed myself to get ahead of myself."

In 1981, Kelly and his family traveled to New York in order to attend the NBA draft. "I was projected anywhere from four to fourteen," he said. "After the (New Jersey) Nets passed on me at ten, a hometown guy, I really thought I was going to go to (Washington). I'm getting ready to get up, and all of a sudden they take Frank Johnson, a guard out of Wake Forest, and I thought, *Wow, that's interesting.* Then Detroit was next at twelve. I think Utah was next at thirteen. I'm going, *I know I don't want to go to Utah,*" he added. "I remember looking real quickly at the Detroit table and seeing this baldheaded chubby guy. I don't know who this guy is, he just points at me, like, you're going to be the one," he stated. Kelly heard his name announced by the Detroit Pistons, which was the twelfth overall NBA pick. "I was surprised, because I had not talked to anybody (from Detroit)," he said. "They were the worst team in the league. They hadn't won anything. The only thing I knew was that I was going to be teammates with Isiah Thomas, because he was taken on the second pick," he added. Ironically, this wasn't the first time a Tripucka would play a professional sport in Detroit. Kelly's father, Frank Tripucka, was a quarterback for the Detroit Lions thirty-two years earlier.

As a rookie for the lowly Pistons, Kelly immediately made his presence known. "I was a starter from the get-go," he stated. "I averaged over twenty points a game and made the All-Star team my first year. That was huge to make it as a rookie," he added. "I was out to prove everybody wrong. I was scared, I was nervous, but I was confident, too."

As time went on, Kelly learned from the good and bad experiences that started from his very first NBA exhibition game. "I got about eight of my shots blocked," he exclaimed. "Welcome to the NBA. That game taught me more than anything else. More than anything, I learned, and I was persistent even though I got my shots blocked. I had to go back in there and do it again. I learned how to get my shot off," he added. "You learn. You take experiences from bad situations, good situations, and try to improve and work on them."

Kelly experienced a lot of personal and professional highlights during his five seasons in Detroit. "There were just so many," he stated. "Greektown, super fans, you know, a work in progress. You're playing in a football arena, the Silverdome, on a makeshift basketball court. They didn't get anybody in, like 5,000 people there the year before when they lost all of those games. Working to get better as a player and to get better as a team. (Isiah) and I, we had to inflict some juice into this team," he admitted. "Anything we had to do to get people in the stands, we did. It was old school. We used to think up promotion nights. There were so many. We did a toga night. I had to do a commercial wearing a toga," he laughs. "Whenever they wanted to promote something to get people to come to the game (they'd say), 'Hey, let's go and ask Kelly. He'll do it.' And I would!"

Despite the commercial and courtside antics that focused on filling the stands, Kelly remained focused on one thing... Winning. "I think that was part of the reason why we were drafted," he said while also referring to Isiah. "We wanted to win! I don't want to lose (and) in that regard, I knew Isiah was a lot like me. That's all you ever want to do, as far as I was concerned. That's number one!"

During the summer of 1986, Kelly was traded to the Utah Jazz. "Worst day of my life," he stated. "Never saw it coming. (I) was completely disappointed, shocked. That tore me apart more than anything, I think, to this day," he added. "I found out at a golf tournament, which is not the way you want to find out. Somebody overheard a TV report; they didn't know I was at a locker in the next aisle. It was terrible. I was completely devastated!" he exclaimed. "I was comfortable in Detroit. I thought we were very close to being very, very good. We had been in the playoffs three straight years. I didn't want to go to Utah. As it turned out, after I got traded (Detroit) ended up winning (the NBA Championship) two years in a row. It was the worst two years in my life. It was very difficult on my wife. It was difficult physically on me, as well. I got sick a couple of times. I wasn't even playing the second year, I was sitting on the end of the bench. It was just miserable," he added.

Kelly's reprieve would come in 1988 during the NBA expansion draft with a transaction between the Charlotte Hornets, who were an NBA expansion team, and the Utah Jazz. "I (actually) didn't get taken in the expansion, they ended up trading for me," he said. "The sun came out. (I was) just feeling like the weight of the world was off me." Not only did this trade put some renewed life into his game, it allowed Kelly to set some new records. "I scored the first point in Charlotte's history, I had the first steal, I had the first three-pointer," he boasted. Kelly played in over seventy-five games a season, on the average, during the next three years in Charlotte. Every one of those games was a battle as they scratched and dug just to compete. Despite losing more games than they won, Kelly felt like they were always treated like champions. "At the end of the year we had a parade through downtown Charlotte," he said. "It was like a World Championship Parade."

Unfortunately, things in Charlotte began to change after those three seasons. "The inmates were running the asylum," he proclaimed. "Some of the kids started acting like they were bigger than the game. They fired (Coach) Dick Carter. They hired a new general manager. Things changed dramatically," he added. "(My) minutes are down, not having as much fun, my role changed. I knew that if there was a transition period, I could be a great guy off the bench. I am going to be a free agent and I would still like to come back. Two of my kids were born there, I really established some roots," he exclaimed. "And they never gave me an offers sheet, never offered me anything."

Even though the door to Charlotte was now closed, Kelly remained optimistic that other playing options would develop. "I figured someone will pick me up," he said. "I still thought I could play another two or three years." As the summer passed Kelly was still without an NBA offer, so he made a rash decision. To this day, it is a decision that he still regrets. "My agent had gotten (me) an offer overseas," he said. "He thought it was a good deal for me and the money was good. I was going over to France." Partway through the European season Kelly experienced a knee injury that required surgery. During this time, the coach was fired and the replacement did not see eye-to-eye with Kelly. "It ended up being a bad experience," he said. "I regret it to this day, because I didn't get back into the NBA."

In 1992, Kelly's hope to play in the NBA again turned into a possible reality when he received word that he would be called to a rookie camp with the New Jersey Nets. Unfortunately, his hope soon turned into disappointment. "I'm sitting at home going, 'I'm going to go to training camp,'" he said. "I'll be darned if they didn't call and didn't invite me. So basically, that was it. That's how it ended. I was getting ready to go to camp, and the next thing you know, I'm not going to camp," he added. "It got quiet. You're going, 'What am I going to do?' I was just thinking, *Well, that might be it. I've got to start thinking about the retirement word. As much as I don't like it, what am I going to do?'*

Kelly reflected on his days with the Detroit Pistons and the positive experience he had doing commercials on radio and TV. "I was always interested in broadcasting," he stated. "I remember making some phone calls and they all were telling me, you need to get some experience. I came back (to New Jersey) and found some work with a couple of different people on the college level. Doing some local games, small conferences along the East Coast," he said. "I was doing those games and it was fun, but I was really interested in the NBA. There was something I read in the paper that said Mike Fratello was getting a job coaching, back into the NBA, so he was going to have to leave his (broadcasting) post in Detroit. I called my longtime friend and said, I want that job! He gave me the job. I started my broadcasting with George Blaha," he added.

Doing the Pistons' broadcasts kept Kelly on an NBA schedule and rubbing shoulders with players and coaches, but it didn't alleviate his desire to play at the professional level. "I still wanted to play," he exclaimed. "It never really goes away. You feel like you can still do it. I still see it when I call games," he added.

After broadcasting for eights seasons in Detroit, Kelly received an enticing offer. "I had a big break," he said. "It was difficult for me to leave, but it was an opportunity you couldn't refuse. I was offered a job doing the Nets games on radio, which meant all eighty-two games. The money was better. I thought this was a great opportunity and there was opportunity because the Nets were thinking about starting a new (TV) network. There might be an opportunity to get back into television. So I left TV to go do radio because of the fact that it was more money, a chance to do all of the games, and be (based) at home," he added. "As much as I was sad to leave and enjoyed my time with the Pistons (and) for eight years with George, it's something I think anybody would have done."

As suspected, the opportunity for Kelly to get back into television back home came after completing one season on the radio. "They offered me the job," he stated. From 2002 until 2005, Kelly would broadcast every Nets game, except for those contracted with national television. Following the fourth season, things began to turn against Kelly. "It turned out that our contracts were up and they brought in a new owner. He didn't bring us back," he said. "They ended up hiring Marv Albert. So I lost my job."

Kelly found himself sitting at home the following full season and wasn't sure what he was going to do. "I've got nothing to do, and I have no idea," he said. "These (broadcast) jobs are hard to come by, because there is only one in every city as far as basketball, and I just can't pick up and move (because of my family)," he added. "I'm sitting at home and I don't know what to do with myself."

In the fall of 2006, Kelly received a phone call that would change his uncertainty. "Around October, I got a phone call out of the blue from Isiah Thomas," he said. "My wife answered the phone and says, 'It's Isiah,' and I say, 'What the hell does he want?' He read about (my release) in the paper and said, 'You've got the groove, but you can't sit at home; you got to do something. Why don't you come work for me?' I said, 'What do you want me to do?' and he says, 'Well, I don't know. Let's feel it out, but in the meantime, why don't you scout?' (So now) I'm an NBA personnel guy, scouting personnel," he stated. "I was an announcer for twelve years, I know all of the teams, and I know the players, so I'm looking at personnel in case of trades or free agency. That's what I've been doing now for the last year. I ended up (broadcasting) two Pistons games in the playoffs, I got permission to do it and went back to work with George. It was a ball! It was tremendous, I miss it. I really do miss it," he added. "But I enjoy what I am doing. I'm thankful, more than I can even tell you, that Isiah called me and did what he did," he said. "That shows you the type of friendship we've had the last twenty-five years. What type of person he is, regardless of how they portray him in the media now."

Kelly appreciates the opportunities he's had because of basketball. "I (am) fortunate," he exclaimed. "I lived most people's dream. Starting from high school, through college, and professionally. I made good money, I made a good living, but in the end nothing lasts forever. I'm still the same guy that I was when I played," he stated. "Basketball was just what I did, not who I was. I was famous; I'm still famous to some people. You've got to be more than that. Now, you've got to be a father, you've got to be a husband, you've got to be a teacher, you've got to be a man of many hats. You've got to be able to accept and overcome and deal with the good and bad," he added. "Ups and downs, life goes on. You've still got to fight and claw, you've still got to go out and get up in the morning and find something to do and find something you like, and if you don't like it, keep searching. That's what I kind of feel like, I'm still searching. We still want to live our past and still do the things that I said before, that our mind thinks we can do, but our body can't. I miss the competition more than anything else," he stated. "I miss that so much, because it's what you were raised on, it's what you were paid to do; it's what you played for. You can't replace it! I'm telling you, there is no way! Anybody that says they can, they're either lying or don't know what they're talking about. I really don't think you can ever replace the competition. That's just a fact of life," he claims.

Every day, Kelly attempts to fulfill his competitive edge. "I'm a very, very competitive person," he states. "Golf, that's kind of become my passion. (It) is such a difficult sport. It is something like the rabbit chasing the carrot... You never get it. It's not so much the competition, it's a challenge, to better yourself," he clarifies. "You challenge yourself. You've got to have something to do. You've got to keep your mind busy and your body busy," he added. Perhaps, Kelly will someday catch that elusive carrot while attempting to fulfill his competitive edge, but in the meantime, it's clear that Kelly Tripucka won't tolerate anything short of excellence while facing his most challenging opponent, which is TIME. "It sucks to get old," he concluded.

Chapter 9
DAVE BING

Dave Bing was a high school and collegiate All-America basketball player. As a #1 draft-pick by the Detroit Pistons in 1966 he went on to be an eight-time NBA All-Star during his twelve professional seasons. Dave became the first Piston to ever have his number retired, was inducted into the NBA Hall of Fame in 1990, and was named one of the top 50 Basketball Players of All Time.

Dave Bing is the epitome of success in many aspects of his life. He's accrued a multitude of honors as a high school, collegiate, and professional athlete, and built an industrial empire, *The Bing Group,* thereafter...but it didn't just happen.

The athletic success began for Dave as a member of the basketball team at Spingarn High School in Washington, DC. His team won the City Championship his junior and senior years and accumulated a three-year record of 64-7, which he attributes to a good supporting cast. "We had seven players on our team that averaged double figures (in scoring)," he stated. "So we were always pretty balanced, and I was a top scorer, averaging about nineteen (points) a game. Nineteen a game is not what we would call a stellar stat, but was because of the talent that I had around," he added. Dave's basketball accomplishments were stellar enough to be noticed as he was selected to the All-America team and went on to attend Syracuse University on a basketball scholarship.

It was at Syracuse that he began to understand just how good he could be and stated, "That's when I realized that I was a pretty good player because I had never basically been out of the city of Washington, DC. You're (now) playing against guys from all over the country and it became clear to me that I could really play," he added. "I started averaging twenty-five, twenty-six points a game as a freshman (and) couldn't play varsity because back then you had to play (on the) freshman (team). As my class moved up to the varsity, the Syracuse program really started to turn around. It culminated in my senior year, when we lost to Duke in the regional finals. I averaged twenty-nine points a game as a senior and our team averaged 100 points, which is unbelievable!" he exclaimed. As Dave was experiencing many individual and team successes at Syracuse, he started to think about his athletic life after college. "You're playing against pretty talented people from all over the country," he said. "As I continued to develop, I started playing against pros and could hold my own against (them). That's when I knew I had a chance to go to the next level."

Dave became the #1 draft pick of the Detroit Pistons and was chosen #2 overall in the 1966 NBA draft. He had an immediate impact and won the NBA Rookie of the Year Award, which he followed up with an individual scoring championship his second season. Despite these achievements, Dave admitted that his entry into the NBA wasn't easy and it took a lot of work, as well as a change in the team's style of play. "It was a tough transition!"

he stated emphatically. "When I got here Tommy Van Arsdale and Eddie Miles were both big, strong guards. They were both six foot five, 220 pounds and yet I came in at six foot three, 185 pounds. When we were playing (a) half court (style of basketball) they would just physically beat you. I was glad when we started playing full court, because neither one of them could keep up with me," he added. "At half court, being quick doesn't matter." Individually, Dave enjoyed the up-tempo style of play but looked to accomplish more as a team. "I never played on a really good team my first five or six years in Detroit," he said. "From an individual standpoint, there were a lot of things, but as in any team sport the whole goal is to try to win a championship."

As his years in the NBA continued he started to realize that his body began to change, and this, combined with a serious eye injury during the course of his fifth season, caused a shift in his way of thinking. "Once you get by thirty, thirty-two years old your body starts to change," he said. "I wasn't a physical specimen, the seven-foot guy that plays fifteen, sixteen years. A guy my size, once you start losing a step or two in quickness it starts to have an effect on your overall game, and I could see that happening, so I had to change my style of play. I didn't worry about scoring as much, I had to become more of a complete player, a true point guard," he added. "In my fifth year I had a detached retina. That was the beginning of the change I went through. I was averaging twenty-five, twenty-six points a game between year two and year six (but) after that injury, where my doctors basically said, 'You should think about retiring and not play again because if you get re-injured you're going to be blind,' I started thinking differently (and) I played differently at that point."

Despite the fuzzy vision that Dave would experience for the rest of his life, he had a clear vision and foresight about a plan that would prepare him for the transition out of professional basketball. "As I started my tenth, eleventh year it was obvious to me that I had to get ready for a second career," he stated. "I wasn't sure that I'd ever have the chance to coach or manage so I made the most of my time by trying to prepare myself so if I couldn't stay in basketball, I was able to do something else," he added. "I worked in the off-season. My first seven years with National Bank in Detroit as a management trainee and then the next two years I worked with the Chrysler Corporation getting exposed to the dealer program (and marketing). I was fortunate enough and had the foresight to work in the off-season as opposed to do nothing, (like) maybe play golf, or go on speaking engagements, or whatever. I learned another trade," he stated.

Even though Dave positioned himself to work and acquire knowledge as he prepared for his exit from professional basketball, there was something that was still missing from his résumé of accomplishments; an NBA championship. After leaving the Pistons Dave spent two seasons with his hometown Washington Bullets and then looked to retire, but a certain connection from his youth brought him back to the game. "Red Auerbach still lived in Washington, DC," he said. "We had known each other for a long time, since I was twelve years old. He talked me out of retirement, and I went up to the (Boston) Celtics. The Celtics had a good team, so I went there with the idea of trying to play on a championship team," he shared. "The money that you were making or all of your personal statistics, it didn't matter. It was about trying to play on a championship team!" he exclaimed. "Well, what happened is that (John) Havlichek announced his retirement, Dave Collins decided that he had had enough and was becoming a cab driver, Charlie Scott got traded for Don Chaney, who was injured and couldn't play, and JoJo White tore his Achilles tendon. All of the bad things that could've happened seemed to happen that year. It was obvious to me that I didn't want to go back at thirty-four years old, on a team that was going to rebuild without Havlichek," he stated. "I had another year on my contract, but I made up my mind that I wasn't going back. I wasn't ready at thirty-four to just continue to flop around and pad my statistics. After twelve years, I'd accomplished what I needed to accomplish, with the exception of playing on a championship team," he added.

In 1978, Dave Bing walked away from the game of basketball and moved on to the next phase of his life. This transition was expected and even prepared for, but it still came with an emotional struggle and a void. "You lose the camaraderie that you've built with you teammates," he stated. "It's hard to explain unless you've been an athlete," he added. "You spend so much time together; be it practice, be it games, be it traveling, be it socially, whatever the case may be. We spent a lot of time together and therefore got to know each other very well, so that's what you miss, in my opinion, more than anything else. Without a doubt, the biggest void that you'd have would be the relationships with your teammates." In addition to the emotional struggle Dave experienced a practical one as an entrepreneur, as well. "The most difficult thing is when I decided to go into business by myself," he shared. "Because being an ex-jock, being an African-American, in most cases people would say that that's an advantage, but I don't think anybody took me very seriously when I first came out and said I wanted to start my own business. I had laid the groundwork; the foundation was in place both from a financial and marketing standpoint. I trained for two years prior to starting my own company in 1980, but the most difficult thing was as an athlete you're spoiled because everybody wants a piece of you. As an ex-player I went out and let people know that I'm starting my business. Nobody took it seriously," he added.

Though Dave felt that being an ex-professional athlete hindered how seriously others took him, he personally discovered an advantage to his sports background. "I think by having been an athlete, especially in team sports, you're taught that you don't get too high and excited about your wins and your personal accomplishments, or too low about your losses," he said. "You try as best you can to keep an even keel towards sports and I think that's helped me in business so that when people slam the door on you and say, 'We don't have time for you,' you didn't give up, you didn't quit, (and) you're ready to go back." Even with this tenacious attitude, Dave experienced some fear shortly after leaving basketball. "I never made the big dollars," he stated. "In my era, the big dollars weren't available, but making six figures, whether it's $200,000 or $300,000, at that time was very, very good money. But going into the real world and having a job where that wasn't accessible to you (like) the first year I got into business. A lot of the savings that I had accrued to put into the business was lost in a very short period of time and there was a huge fear of failure," he admitted. "(I) had to adjust and make a decision as to whether I'm going to stick with this or do something different. I made the decision to continue in the business, and it's worked out very well. I'm in my twenty-seventh year at this point." Many would agree that "very well" may be an understatement when looking at the long list of individual and business accomplishments Dave has acquired since leaving professional basketball. As Chairman of *The Bing Group,* he has built a base of over 600 employees with gross sales of over $500 million annually. His company has been chosen seven times as a Supplier of the Year by his customers. In 1984, Dave was honored by President Reagan at the White House as the National Minority Small Business Person of the Year. He has received lifetime achievement awards, Business Newsmaker of the Year, community involvement awards, humanitarian awards, and two honorary graduate degrees. Dave serves on the Board of Directors for Detroit Renaissance, the Economic Club of Detroit, Michigan Minority Business Development Council, National Association of Black Automotive Suppliers, and the University Preparatory Academy. He is a board advisor for Detroit Black United Fund, Boys and Girls Club of Southeastern Michigan, Junior Achievement, and the Boy Scouts of America. He is a Trustee for the McGregor Fund and the University of Detroit Mercy. Despite his unbelievable involvement and great accomplishments, Dave remains humble and appreciates the people who have worked to assist in his success. "The greatest satisfaction that I get today is that I know that I'm responsible for the livelihood of a lot of families, and that's important (to me)," he added. Dave also takes great pride in his own family and their involvement with his work. "All three of my daughters are college graduates," he exclaimed. "They're all working in the business (and) I'm very proud of them. They're not spoiled to the point where they think that they're just supposed to get the benefits. They all go to work every day, and they're effective at what they do," he added.

Looking back at Dave Bing's long list of athletic and business accomplishments solidifies the legacy of success he will leave. He has shown that with hard work, a willingness to learn, and a tenacity to never give up, people can overcome much and accomplish their goals. There is no question that Dave Bing will have success at whatever endeavor he chooses, and he has a track record to prove it.

Chapter 10
ALLAN HOUSTON

The Detroit Pistons drafted Allan Houston in 1993. He played in the NBA for twelve seasons and was considered one of the league's all-time greatest long-range shooters. Allan was an NBA All-Star twice and given the Good Guys in Sports Award four times by The Sporting News. *He also represented our country on Team USA in the 2000 Olympics and won a gold medal.*

Few athletes have experienced the benefit of having a parent who possessed a set of gym keys. With a father who was a former collegiate athlete and then a collegiate coach, Allan Houston all but possessed the gym, let alone the keys. Since a very young age Allan could be found around the University of Louisville campus, where his father was an assistant basketball coach for thirteen years. "My life was kind of built around basketball," he stated. "Always traveling with the team, I learned a lot from them. Basketball was pretty much our life," he added.

Allan participated in track and field while attending Ballard High School in Louisville, but displayed his main talent in basketball when he led his team to a state championship in 1988. Following high school, Allan signed a letter of intent with the University of Louisville but got released in order to attend the University of Tennessee after his father was named their new head coach. "He got the job after I signed with Louisville," he stated. "I was able to go to Tennessee without being penalized. There was no other person I would rather play for," he added.

Allan's successes in basketball continued at Tennessee and included many highlights. "Just playing for my dad," he exclaimed. "Being a freshman and being able to start. We played against some very intense, athletic and very tough teams. My sophomore year we made it to the championship game in the SEC tournament," he added. "I got the MVP of the tournament." By the time Allan left college he earned first team All-SEC each of his four years, was a two-time All-America selection, and became Tennessee's all-time leading scorer with 2,801 points. He had thoughts of playing basketball at the next level, but not initially. "I didn't really think about playing in the NBA, honestly, until probably after my sophomore year," he said. "I heard a couple of people asking around, like is Allan going to stay four years. (It) never crossed my mind. I just wanted to just be as good as I could, and help my dad out and try and win," he shared. "I just remember going on my knees in prayer and having my parents, just talking to them. I remember God saying not too many people get this opportunity to play for their dad and graduate in four years. I just wanted to have one more year of that experience of playing for my dad," he added.

After finishing his degree in African-American Studies and his collegiate basketball career, Allan was drafted by the Detroit Pistons in 1993. "Being in Detroit, I think it was cool because I think people were excited about Lindsay Hunter and I coming and kind of playing up under Joe (Dumars) and Isiah (Thomas)," he said. "It was exciting for me because I got to learn a lot from those guys. I learned a lot about how they treated the game, and the work ethic, and how professional they were. They really set the tone for me and my career," he exclaimed.

Behind the likes of Dumars and Thomas, Allan saw limited playing time his first year and a half in Detroit but still found a way to stay in shape. "I remember nights when I would go to the Franklin Racquet Club after practice just because I wasn't getting any time," he said. "I was probably risking injury and everything, but I thought, *I've got to keep my skills sharp.* I remember that it was a challenge, but I remember my father always had a positive outlook on situations. He told me, 'Just look at this way, you're adding another year to your career.' I didn't get it at the time, but when I got into my tenth year, I looked back and was like, (he) knew what he was talking about."

Following Allan's third season in Detroit, he signed as a free agent with the New York Knicks. "I really wanted to stay and expected to stay," he stated. "I really expected the Pistons to want me, too, and it just didn't work out that way. That was probably one of the most challenging parts in my career, leaving Detroit," he said. "It seemed like the Pistons made it look like it was me wanting to go, when they kind of made that business decision. I kept thinking that you're with these guys, they're family, they're friends, and then at some point you're going to experience the business side of it. That's what it was and not really personal," he added.

As he headed to New York, Allan realized that this was a critical point in his career. "There comes a point where you're going to be challenged because of circumstances around you," he said. "You can't really give up on your goals and faith in who you are and what you can do. I always thought that I could be a good player in this league. I just remember always believing that there was going to be a time when I was going to be able to do what I've been doing, and I just worked," he exclaimed. "It really was an adjustment, but I thank God and my parents (because) through my upbringing I have inner strength to just deal with it and just continue to work. I just worked and worked and eventually as a team we experienced some success in the playoffs. Playing the playoffs in New York, there's just nothing else like it," he exclaimed. "New York fans are like your wife; they'll let you know when you're doing well and they'll let you know when you're doing badly, too," he joked.

When it came to handling the intense pressure that comes with being an elite player in New York and the NBA, Allan credits his deep faith. "I was introduced at a young age to my faith," he said. "When you have that foundation, you have a perspective that life is not about you, and that this is a game and a tool that you've been blessed with to use. So many people put so much stock in a game or a season or what someone else thinks about you," he added. "The reality is that God loves every one of us, no matter how we perform and what we do. So that's why I was like, if I can please God, then that's my focus," he exclaimed. "At the end of the day you're a competitor, you obviously want to please your teammates, your coaches, your fans, and you want to live up to your own expectations, but my focus was really to make sure that I lived with strong character," he added. "I was glad that I learned from my parents and the people around me that character is the biggest, the most important thing. I think over the long haul, that's what people will appreciate about any of us is that no matter how many points we score (or) MVP awards (we acquire), what I think people will remember the most is who we are as people and the legacy we leave."

As Allan began to depart from professional basketball a

legacy was already being left on the court. During his twelve seasons he was touted as one of the purest shooters in the NBA, finishing his career as one of the all-time greatest long-range shooters and one of the all-time leading scorers in Knicks history. Allan was a two-time NBA All-Star and in his last healthy season, finished as the tenth leading scorer in the league. He also played on Team USA and won a Gold Medal in the 2000 Olympics. Despite these accomplishments, his departure from basketball did not come without a struggle. During the course of his final two seasons Allan incurred micro-fractures in his knees, first his left and then his right. "I'd gone through about a year and a half of battling, getting back, and I finally realized that the only way I was going to be able to play is if I just took some time off, and just let my body heal," he said. "My contract situation, the pressures of playing under contract, and all of that wasn't going to allow it. Those were the highest years of my deal. I wasn't going to go in there and say that I need some time off. It just wasn't realistic for the management of the team. They did a lot, they really did everything they could to help me back, but what was needed was just time away. I just realized and I just felt a peace about retiring," he exclaimed. "And once I had that peace I was like, it's time. I told Coach Brown, I told Isiah, I talked to the team, and we had a press conference. I think people were kind of glad to see that all of this stuff was over, with me trying to figure out if I'm coming back," he added. Allan knew that if it weren't for his injuries he would still be playing. "I always felt like I still had something left to offer," he said. "My best year was my last healthy year, in 2003."

In 2005, Allan left the hustle and bustle of professional basketball and he had no problem finding other things to do with his time. In fact, he simply enjoyed the time. "I think the first year I was just happy to be off," he shared. "I took trips with my dad and played golf. It was more of a relief," he added. "I was just happy to have my own time, make my own schedule, go to Thanksgiving, go to Christmas, and I hadn't been able to do that in thirty years." Allan was also able to devote more time to the Allan Houston Foundation, which focuses on serving the needs of youth in many ways. "I really feel led to have an impact on this generation any way I can, I just felt like that's been my calling," he stated. "With my foundation me and my dad hold a father/son basketball camp where we really give fathers and sons tools to become stronger children and men," he said. "(We) use the game of basketball and give them spiritual tools, too, because a good father can't be a father that he can potentially be unless he's connected to The Father. I see lives changed," he added. In 2007, Allan's fatherhood was recognized as the National Fatherhood Initiative honored him with the "Father of the Year" Award.

From his own father, Allan inherited a strong entrepreneurial spirit and he continues to build Allan Houston Enterprises, which serves as an umbrella company for a variety of business ventures that include a media and entertainment company, as well as an urban fashion producer licensed by the NBA (UNK), and another potential clothing venture on the rise. "One of my goals is to be a strong businessman," he said. "I was fortunate enough to have parents who supported and taught me good and very valuable life lessons," he added.

At thirty-five years of age and retired from the NBA, Allan has a whole life ahead of him, but there are aspects of the game that he still misses. "What I honestly miss the most is the rush," he stated. "There's an emotional high you get from making a shot, making a play, the competitiveness that goes into it. Playing and winning a game, I don't know if there will ever be anything that matches that type of quick power high. The risk/reward is so high," he added. "I really miss the interaction with the crowd.

The biggest thing I hear people say all of the time is, 'Man, I miss that jump shot,' I hear it every day and I'm saying in my heart, *I miss it too,"* he exclaimed. "You know, above everything else, just displaying a gift that you've been given." What made Allan's transition even more difficult was that he was not able to depart on his conditions. "The biggest challenge for me is giving up something that (I) didn't feel was on (my) terms," he said. "(I) felt like (I) still had something to give, but (I) just couldn't give it."

Now Allan fortunately gains tremendous enjoyment from spending time with his family. He is happily married to Tamara and has three wonderful children. "I get so much fulfillment from being around my family," he exclaimed. "A lot of people say (they) miss the camaraderie, (they) miss the locker room, I miss that, but I get so much more from being around my family and kids that I don't really think about that much." He also enjoys the fact that he can now be in control of his own schedule. "Besides working for ESPN, (I) don't really have to be anywhere where you're going to be fined," he joked. "Being thirty-five and being able to do that is a blessing. If I want to take a class, if I want to travel, if I want to play golf and work out and go play, I can do those things. Don't stop that routine," he advises when referring to his workouts. "Make sure you're physically healthy, spiritually healthy, all of those different areas." Allan's own spiritual health has kept him grounded and provided clear direction for his life. "We can have so many different things that we're able to do because of the platform we've been given," he said. "It makes it even more important for us to have a clear-set plan and goal, and only God can really give us that. That's the one thing that really helped me, because I've had to say no to a lot of things. Only God knows your purpose and what you were created in existence to do before you were born. He is the one that puts that desire in our hearts, it's not something that we just make up," he added.

"Unless we're constantly connected, it's like a radio station—if you're not dialed in then you're going to hear static. If you're dialed in, then you're going to clearly hear the message on the radio."

Allan may not know every single detail of his future at this time but it is clear that he is enjoying every moment. Every moment that he is able to spend time with his family, every moment that he is able to reach out and serve the next generation of youth, and every moment that he is able to physically heal and display the athletic gift he has been given. Allan Houston may never hit another jump shot again on an NBA court, but he is dialed in on following his heart and living a very purposeful life, which many agree will be as impacting off the court as it was on, if not more so.

Chapter 11
BILL GADSBY

Bill Gadsby was the second player in NHL history, along with longtime friend Gordie Howe, to have a twenty-year NHL career. As a Hall of Fame athlete, Bill was known for his rough and tumble play that reportedly landed him over 600 stitches throughout his tenure. In addition to his lengthy playing career, which placed him in Chicago, New York, and ultimately Detroit, Bill Gadsby had the opportunity to coach the Red Wings, as well.

Raised in Calgary, Alberta, Bill Gadsby had an interest in many sports. Active in basketball and football, it would be hockey that brought him the most rewards at Preston Heights High School, when he received the team's MVP award. He later clarified which sport would soon reign when he was given the opportunity to move to Edmonton in order to play in a developmental hockey league while finishing high school. "I liked hockey better than I did the other sports," he said. "I enjoyed playing football, I think it was the contact as it is in hockey." As fate would have it, Bill's association with the Detroit Red Wings would already evolve despite the fact that he was still in high school at the time. His current developmental coach in Edmonton also scouted western Canada for the Red Wings.

In the spring of 1946, Bill finished high school and progressed further into the world of hockey at this point. "You'd play for a sponsored team when you became the age to turn pro, which was eighteen," he said. "They owned you. Nothing like it is today, where there's a draft." Bill's team was sponsored by the Chicago Blackhawks and after a brief stint with their Minor League team in Kansas City, he was called up to Chicago, where he reportedly signed an NHL contract for $7,500 with an additional $3,000 signing bonus. Bill spent the next nine seasons with the Blackhawks and credits his success to his previous coach in Edmonton. "I had some good tutoring," he said. "I had a coach that last year I played (in Edmonton) that played in the NHL, so when Chicago came with the general manager, owner, and coach to Edmonton to interview me about turning pro, I got a lot of inside information from (my coach), who had been through that."

Another familiar name, Gordie Howe, joined the professional hockey ranks the very same year as Bill. While Bill was blossoming from the Minor League in Kansas City to the Chicago Blackhawks, Gordie Howe was advancing through the ranks of the Detroit Red Wings organization. "I didn't really know him then (but) I just had lunch with him today," he said. From those early days their relationship has grown, primarily because of the fact that they shared twenty years in the NHL, and Bill's final five seasons together on the Red Wings. Gordie and Bill weren't the first to play twenty years in the league, though. "Gordie and I were the second guys to play twenty years," he stated. "A guy in Boston, named Dit Clappler, played twenty years and (up to that point) he was the only one. When I was in Chicago and the

Boston Bruins came into town every team was honoring (Clapper) for his twenty years. I wasn't even born when he played his first year," Bill added. "He said to me on the ice that night, 'Son, I hope you can last as long as I did. That would be nice.' I was eighteen years old and oh, my gosh," Bill exclaimed with excitement.

"I really enjoyed the game. I thought it had everything: speed, and finesse, and body contact," he said. "It was a hell of a life for me." Bill became quite well known amongst the NHL for his financial wizardry, especially when it came to something called "stitch insurance." Apparently, the players would pay a nominal fee for an insurance policy that paid a player for every stitch he received, reportedly up to $5 a stitch. It didn't take long before Bill became wise and made more than the premiums he paid. Often players would even ask their doctor to put the stitches closer together, in order to gain an extra one or two each time. Despite many injuries, including broken bones and reportedly over 600 stitches, Bill didn't think beyond hockey or what he might do when his final playing days were over until late in his career. "Probably, around the nineteenth or twentieth year," he said. "I felt if I was playing well I could keep going. Didn't give it much thought about what I was going to do. Didn't really know what I was going to do," he added. "(It) was the twentieth year and we got beat out by the Canadians in the finals. I had had enough," he stated. "I told my wife something when we lost that last game. I came off the ice and I said, 'Honey, you seen me play my last game.' I told her that night I had just had enough."

In 1966, Bill gave up his skates, but remained on the ice in another capacity. "I got the opportunity to go back to Edmonton and coach the junior league team," he said. "That was big-time junior hockey in Canada then." As a member of the Western Canada Junior League, it didn't take long before Bill was reminded of the difference between the NHL and junior league hockey. That reminder came in the form of a road trip that his young team would take north of Manitoba. "We went there twice a year," he stated. "We would fly to Winnipeg and then take the bus, which is like seven hours. It's 30, 40 below, I mean, 30, 40 below. That was an experience after coming out of the National Hockey League and then you're on a bus and freezing your ass off," he added. "It's different. What really got to me was how many mistakes the kids were making the first couple of months. Giving the puck away, running at the guys that they shouldn't be running at because you're going to miss them, you know, a lot of mistakes and bad passing. We had to bring that from the NHL because the kids are only sixteen, seventeen, eighteen years old. That was tough to get it through their heads," he shared. Bill also discovered a major difference between playing and coaching. "You get behind the fence in a hockey game before it starts or even that afternoon (and) you get those butterflies," he said. "I used to get them when I played but once the puck was dropped I was fine. Not when you're coaching, it's more of a bitch when you're coaching. When you're a player you can get on the ice out there and you can knock somebody on their ass and you feel a little better. Can't do that when you're on the bench," he exclaimed. "You see some of those coaches now and I think they're going to have a heart attack."

Following two seasons in Edmonton, Bill was faced with another opportunity, when the Red Wings called him and asked him to coach. His decision to take the Red Wings head coaching position wasn't necessarily based on any unhappiness in Edmonton, but perhaps another chance at fleeting glory. "I was happy in Edmonton and we were settled in," he said. "To make another move, especially with four kids in school, that was a tough decision to make, but when you get a chance to coach in the NHL, just the honor, it makes you feel good inside," he stated, acknowledging this as the selling point for this return to Detroit.

Initially excited and optimistic, Bill's NHL coaching career took a bad turn at the beginning of his second season. "I was fired after winning the first two games," he stated. "One of the biggest shocks in my life was getting fired. It hurt me in a lot of ways. We went to Chicago (and won), we beat Toronto here and we were going back to Chicago the next night. We beat them and Bruce Norris, the owner, had his arm around me in the dressing room after the game and said, 'Boy, Bill, you really got these guys going' and I said, 'You're going to have a good year, Bruce." From that brief interaction, Bill thought things were well and that the club was looking good, but the following proved those thoughts wrong. "What hurt me was the night before giving me all this bullshit," he stated "That was pretty hard to take." What made this event even more ironic and difficult to take was the fact that Bill was just freshly inducted into the NHL Hall of Fame.

Following his firing, Bill floundered and was uncertain of a direction he should take. "I didn't know what the hell I was going to do," he exclaimed. "Whether to go back (to Edmonton) or stay here." Fortunately, it didn't take long before another opportunity presented itself; in fact, it was later that night. "Gordie Howe and his wife came home with me that night," he said. "So did another fried, John Crane, who owned JJ Curran Crane Company. He said after a couple of hours of BS-ing, 'I know it's tough, and you don't have to make a decision now, but we'll have lunch in a couple of weeks and I'd like you to come work for me unless you're going to get back into hockey.' And I said, 'Well, right now I don't think I'm going back to something that burns.'" Three days after his firing he received another offer, only this time it was from the owner of the St. Louis Blues, but by then the damage was done.

"I was hurt so dang bad," he shared. "I even told my wife, 'That's it. I'm done with this bullshit, being treated like that.' So (John Crane and I) went and had lunch and I went to work for Curran Crane Company." At forty-three years of age, after being involved with organized hockey for approximately thirty years, Bill was doing something totally different. "I went to all of the construction sites and did a construction report every day as to what's going on and what was built," he said. "I'd go to jobsites, find the superintendent, and give him a price list and bullshit with him a little bit. It's amazing how many guys that either recognized me or thought they did," he added.

Bill's transition from hockey went fairly well, which he attributed to two reasons. The first reason came as a result of the hurt he experienced from being fired, which actually motivated him to let go and move on from hockey. The satisfaction of his new job was the second reason. "I had a hell of a job," he said. "They got me a membership at the Birmingham Country Club. We played a lot of golf with customers. I was there seventeen years," he added. "It's a lot different between sports and the general working conditions, but there wasn't the pressure. If you're not winning it's a hell of a lot of pressure. (Now) it's just like taking a fifty-pound weight off your back. You don't have the butterflies anymore, I was just normal," he stated.

Despite Bill's ability to let go of professional hockey and enjoy his new career, he still missed certain parts of the game. "The camaraderie with the guys, a lot of nice people, fans and what have you," he said. "(But) I had enough after twenty years. The body was beat up pretty good," he added. He eventually found a way to spend time with his old teammates and fans without exerting too much stress on his beat-up body. "I got involved with the Red Wings alumni and we played twenty, twenty-five games a winter, for charity," he said. Bill did this for about twelve years but couldn't remember the last time he donned a pair of skates, as he's now pushing eighty years old.

When it comes to retiring from professional athletics Bill believes there is no set standard for retiring. "Everybody is different, when they should or when they shouldn't," he said. "Go as long as you can as long as you're producing. If you're not and hanging on, that's got to be a bad feeling," he added. "I think I could have played one more year or two but I had enough at that time." When referring to the reason that he has remained in Detroit, Bill stated, "I made the right move going here. My daughter got married here, got grandchildren (here), and we enjoy it here," he said.

Bill Gadsby has come a long way from the rough and tumble reputation, and countless stitches he received as a defenseman. In fact, he is now quite congenial and polite. The title of his autobiographical book, *The Grateful Gadsby*, very appropriately expresses his attitude, which now overflows with gratitude and appreciation for the opportunities he has had in Detroit as result of hockey. "It was a hell of a life, I'll tell you that," he said. "This is a hell of a sports town. It's unreal. It's unbelievable."

Chapter 12
JOHNNY WILSON

Johnny Wilson has won four Stanley Cups while playing for the Detroit Red Wings. He has been involved with professional hockey for over thirty years, which includes coaching the LA Kings, Colorado Rockies, Detroit Red Wings, and Pittsburgh Penguins, in addition to his playing..

Born in Kincardine, Ontario, but spending most of his youth in Rouyn-Noranda, Quebec, there was only one thing Johnny Wilson knew during the cold, long winters. "I started way back in the '40s and at that particular time all the guys did was play hockey because of the cold weather," he said. "It was mostly outdoors because they didn't have the money or facilities. Most large cities in Canada probably had an arena but it was booked solid."

A scout from the Detroit Red Wings became aware of Johnny's talent while he was playing in the Quebec high school provincial championship. "In those days, the system was entirely different," he stated. "You didn't go to a universal draft, they looked at you when you were fifteen, sixteen years old, thinking you might potentially be a National Hockey League player, or participate in the junior program." Johnny added, "In my era, the National Hockey League, which was the original six, sponsored a junior team and that was the spawning ground for the NHL. Every team in the NHL had what they called a glorified junior team, where they would send the fifteen- through eighteen-year-olds as they were finishing their high school education and developing their hockey skills. So the junior teammates that you played with (or) competed against could turn pro," he explained. "The rest of the players might fall by the wayside. At eighteen or nineteen you had a good feel whether you're going to turn pro or not."

While playing junior hockey, Johnny felt he had a bit of an advantage because of the team's location in Windsor, Ontario. "In those days we didn't have video tapes and TV where you could sit back and watch," he said. "We used to go across the river, jump on the Grand River bus, and watch the Red Wings play. My idol was Ted Lindsay," he exclaimed. "I used to watch him because he was a left-winger and Gordie (Howe) and Ted used to come over to Windsor and watch us play on their days off. We all went to training camp together, even at junior, and for the first week we blended in with the pros so we could get more experience. We were bonafide Red Wings when we were seventeen years old and in my era you felt real proud of the fact that they picked you up at seventeen."

By the time Johnny turned twenty years old he would be playing in the NHL. He learned right away that building friendships with opponents was not an option at this level. "There was no fraternizing in my era," he stated. "We didn't give a shit who was out there, you were going to beat them up." This attitude was exemplified by one of the train rides the team would take back and forth from Montreal to Detroit. "We played

Saturday night in Montreal and both teams would jump on the train (for their next destination)," he shared. "We'd have to go through the Canadian car to get to the dining car, so somewhere down the line our team had to walk through their car to go to breakfast. When we sat in the dining room, right on the other side of the dining car might be four Canadian players and on this side might be four Red Wings." Johnny went on to explain that somebody over the years finally put their passenger Pullman cars on each side of the dining car, which was specially fitted with a curtain so that the teams couldn't see each other anymore, especially during the playoffs. "In my era, we played fourteen games against a team, seven home and seven on the road, plus if you played in the playoffs you played a team twenty-one times that year," he said. "You know, you play against a guy four times within a month and you develop a little anger, especially if he might have speared or hit you. Now, NHL players might see each other once or twice a year so you don't have that hatred so to speak because the league is so spread out." He added, "If you nail me now I may not see you until February or March and by that time you could be traded or whatever."

After countless train rides and games, Johnny decided to call it quits. "I played fourteen years in the National Hockey League with Detroit, Chicago, Toronto, and New York," he stated. "Then I retired in New York voluntarily because the money wasn't that good. The athletes in those days didn't make that kind of money. Living in New York and the aggravation of living way out in the suburbs of Long Beach, Long Island, so you could afford to live. Downtown New York rents are too high, so you'd commute and you had about an hour, hour and twenty-five, thirty-five, forty-five minutes, it got longer by car," he added. "Then you stopped at the Daimler expressway, got on the subway, and then another forty minutes on the subway. It became more of a hassle," he exclaimed. In addition, Johnny already had a career established outside of hockey at this time. "I was thirty-four years old and the reason I retired was because I represented Molson Brewery in the summer," he said. "I was making more money at Molson. I had bonuses, I had a car, I had medical, and I had the whole ball of wax. With the Rangers you were the only one insured but if you wife is sick or your family, the NHL wouldn't cover that, it was the players' responsibility," he added. If you were married and your wife gave birth you would receive $300-$400, in Johnny's era. There was a small financial retribution with the infamous "stitch insurance" that some of the players purchased at that time. If a player held one of these policies they could get paid up to $10 for every stitch they incurred. "So if you were cut you'd tell a doctor to put in eight stitches instead of two," he shared. "You'd end up with $80 instead of $20."

With the typical one-year contract prevalent for players in their thirties, and the lack of family insurance coverage, providing more stability for his family outweighed the prestige of playing professional hockey anymore. "I've won four Stanley Cups," he boasted. "I won the honor of playing 580 consecutive games, but when we were in our thirties, they only signed you to a one-year deal. The next year you had to make the team again." Johnny compared this to today's hockey era and stated, "Now, if you're thirty-six and you had a good year they give you a three-year deal. You could play until you're forty." Johnny cites expansion as the main reason for this phenomenon, which allows players sign to play longer today. "There is a demand for players," he states. "(Expansion) is sort of a blend of Minor Leaguers and also Major Leaguers that were phasing out."

Out of professional hockey and now working full time for Molson Brewery, Johnny got sent to Ottawa for three years, primarily because of his bilingual ability. Unable to leave hockey completely, he decided to coach a senior league team and lead them to the league finals. As a result, he was asked by the Canadian Amateur Hockey Association (CAHA) to take his team on a European tour. They were scheduled to play the likes of Russian and Czechoslovakian teams, which because of the current Cold War era was a big deal. However, once the paper work for the trip was submitted and Russia and Czechoslovakia officials saw that a member of the Canadian Mounted Police was on the senior team, they canceled their games. "They figured they would be spying or whatever," he said. "So we had to go play Germany, Sweden, Finland, and Austria instead."

Upon his return, Johnny received a proposition that would draw him further back into the game of hockey. He received a phone call from Bill Jennings, president of the New York Rangers and a Princeton University graduate, who informed him of a varsity hockey coaching vacancy at Princeton, for which he was highly recommended. "I said, 'Well, I'm kind of rooted here and my family and my kids are going to school,'" he stated. "I said, you know, 'I'd have to give it a lot of thought. I've got a pretty good job.'" Following an hour-long phone conversation with Princeton's athletic director Johnny was convinced to take a tour of the campus, where he met the president of the university and was offered a five-year deal. "I said, 'Wow, this ain't all that bad,'" he exclaimed. "I went home, talked to my wife, and ended up calling Molson and retired." Following a third place Ivy League finish Johnny's second year, Princeton was so happy to no longer be the doormat of the league that they destroyed his five-year contract and gave him an indefinite appointment. He could stay as long as he wanted and receive a $1,000 a year raise until he hit $25,000, then they would review it. "So I shook hands, and didn't sign nothing," he stated.

About a month or two following his indefinite appointment at Princeton, Johnny received a phone call from former Maple Leaf teammate and friend Larry Regan. The NHL was in the process of expanding and the LA Kings were interested in having him manage and coach their organization. "I'm really not that interested," he said. "But Larry and I were great buddies, we were teammates in Toronto." So despite having security at Princeton, he decided to take the position with the Kings' organization. Ironically, Johnny discovered that Princeton's men's basketball coach, Butch van Breda Kolff, just accepted an offer to coach the LA Lakers. "So away we went," he stated as he referred to his and Butch's departure to LA. The irony thickened when Butch left to coach the Pistons and Johnny ended up in Detroit with the Red Wings organization. "So we run into one another and he says, 'What are you doing, following me? Or am I following you?' He and I became very good friends, wonderful friends," he shared. "Princeton to LA to Detroit." Despite having the opportunity to go from coaching in the Ivy League to the NHL, for Johnny, it didn't come without some regrets. "If I had to service a monumental error in my life, it's probably leaving Princeton, I could have stayed there," he exclaimed.

From the Red Wings organization Johnny next got involved in the World Hockey Association, but when he discovered that his team in Cleveland might be sold and relocated he took a job with a NHL expansion team. "I was the first coach of the Colorado Rockies," he boasted. After spending only one season with the Rockies, Johnny received another offer. The Pittsburgh Penguins discovered that he only had a one-year contract in Colorado, so they offered him a three-year deal. "So I moved on, I went to Pittsburgh," he stated. "Then I retired after the third year. They wanted to make a coaching change, so I left. I had enough. I was in my early fifties. I came back to Detroit, where

I spent most of my time, got a job, and I've been here ever since," he added. "I worked for Rite-On Industries until they recently closed their doors, went into bankruptcy. I retired from there several months ago."

Johnny is appreciative of his days as a professional player and coach and is well aware of the connections that came as a result. "I did a lot of business because of the fact that I played and coached with the Red Wings," he exclaimed. "Athletes in Detroit are fortunate because people around here put them on a pedestal. It helps open doors," he added. "You go to lobbies and identify yourself and they always had something that if they couldn't help you they would turn you onto somebody else. It was great!"

The countless connections developed because of hockey still couldn't replace the void of its absence. "It's difficult to replace the passion because you develop a passion for the game when you're a kid and you have ambitions, desire, and determination," he stated. "You try to blend that into what your ultimate goal was in life. You have a positive attitude and you develop a thick skin and that helps down the road in business," he said. "Hockey's a physical game and I think out in the business world everybody gets kicked around, you know, disappointments, accomplishments, so you become callused. You develop the kind of character you need when you get out there. You can win eight games and then lose eight games. In business you can be successful in eight or ten quotes but also lose that quote or that job, that's part of being an athlete," he added.

For Johnny, the most difficult part of the transition from professional hockey back into normal, everyday life was the long hours. "You practice an hour and a half a day, you play a sixty-minute game, and you average twenty minutes a game," he stated. "When you work from eight in the morning until four or five in the afternoon, then you have to go back to the office or you have to entertain. When you're playing, the day of your game you're sitting around getting yourself geared up for the game. The game lasts two and a half hours but you only play about twenty minutes," he explained. Johnny also mentioned that in athletics, you typically get immediate feedback, which isn't always the case in business. "As an athlete the owners, coaches, and fans see your results instantly," he said. Johnny misses those instant results as well as the teammates who helped produce them. "When you leave playing, you re-establish whole new relationships," he added.

Johnny doesn't necessarily see eye to eye with today's professional athletes. "I don't understand athletes today," he exclaimed. "Why they run into so many problems, I mean, have they got nothing else to do? Are there too many athletes around? You know, I think maybe when we were small there was more like a humbled aspect to it. Some athletes today don't give a shit about the fans or people," he added.

Now approaching eighty years of age, Johnny still moves and speaks with confidence, as if he's still on the ice, which could be attributed to the fact that he's won four Stanley Cups and has the eternal legacy to prove it. "When you retire they put you on the back burner, but when you win the Cup, your name goes on (it)," he stated. "That's a big difference in what you accomplish in life." When referring to the accomplishment of winning Stanley Cups, Johnny mentions, "Our big parade was from center ice to the dressing room, and we drank out of the Cup. They took the top of the Cup off and put it on the rubbing table and the base stayed downstairs, then we went to the Cadillac Hotel, where we celebrated the four Stanley Cups over the years. We would never see (the Cup) again until we won it," he added. "Now, it's one piece and (the players) can take it anywhere they want. The original one that we drank out of is in Toronto."

Johnny Wilson continues to drink out of his cup of life. "You only go by the board once in life, enjoy every minute," he advises. "You're going to have your ups and downs, but you've got to learn how to blend them, whether it might be financial, marital problems, it's just another day in life. And you as a person have to learn how to handle it; you can't look at somebody else," he concluded. Good advice from someone who has accomplished so much in his life.

Chapter 13
TED LINDSAY

Ted Lindsay played seventeen seasons in the NHL over the course of twenty-one years. He was a first team All-Star eight times and won four Stanley Cups with the Detroit Red Wings. Ted was named NHL Executive of the Year for his work as a general manager in Detroit and was a key catalyst in the organization of the NHL Players Association. In 1966, Ted became a member of the NHL Hall of Fame and had his Red Wings jersey retired in 1991.

Robert Blake Theodore Lindsay, otherwise known as Ted, was a simple man with an uncomplicated philosophy toward life. "Just common sense," he said when describing the basis of this philosophy. Ted grew up in a modest mining town in northern Ontario and was raised by a father who skated in the early 1900s for the equivalent forerunner of the NHL. With six brothers and three sisters Ted could've easily hosted his own neighborhood hockey team, where every third house had a rink in their backyard. It is no surprise that Ted fell in love with hockey from the moment he strapped on his first skates, which were given to him by a neighbor lady and too big because they previously belonged to her husband. "Anytime I could get on the ice, I'd get on the ice," he said. "I was nine years old before I started to skate, which put me in the category of a retarded Canadian," he jokingly added.

At fourteen years of age, Ted competed in his first hockey championship and won the Ontario Championship against future greats Ted Kennedy and Don Ballenger. Following four years of Ontario Junior League hockey, Ted became a Detroit Red Wing at nineteen years of age. He would spend seventeen seasons in the NHL over the course of twenty-one years. Ted's glorious playing career included four Stanley Cups, eight NHL All-Star appearances, and the Art Ross Trophy, which is awarded to the NHL's leading scorer of the season. During these years he had as much impact off the ice, as he was directly involved in organizing the NHL Players' Association.

Ted approached professional hockey one game at a time. "I realized when one game went to two, and two games went to three, and three games went to four, I loved the game and it was taking me and I was following," he said. Standing five foot eight and 160 pounds, Ted was average physical stature but wasn't a pushover on the ice, and had the stitches to prove it. "I had a lot of cuts, well over 600 stitches," he shared. At least he financially profited from these injuries, receiving $10 a stitch from the modest "stitch insurance" many NHL players carried at that time. Ted was no softy off the ice, either, as he placed himself in an adversarial position against the monstrous NHL owners of the time. "I helped form the Players Association," he said. "I didn't want to try to run hockey, but I wanted to be able to sit down and have a voice." As a result, Ted feels three of his seventeen NHL seasons were spent in Chicago playing for the Blackhawks. "I got traded because (I) formed the Players Association," he stated. "I knew something was going to happen, but I didn't know what. I got traded to Chicago and I was still a Red Wing," he said. "I had it tattooed here, tattooed here on my ass, and after two years there, I was (simply) existing, I wasn't living."

In 1995, the Canadian Broadcast Company (CBC) produced a movie titled *Networth,* which depicted Ted's involvement in forming the representation for NHL players. "There was a husband and wife team that wrote a book called *Networth* that covered hockey from the beginning of the '20s until the middle '80s," he said. "In this book, there was one chapter called 'Lindsay's Dream.' When CBC saw the book they had interest in doing a movie made for television on that one chapter."

During his time of playing and off-ice battles with the NHL owners, Ted had the foresight to understand the temporary status of his professional hockey career and started a business with Red Wing teammate Marty Pavolich in 1950. Part of this insight came out of necessity. "When I was single, I'd go back home and sponge off my mom and dad," he said. "You were broke by the time you went back to training camp, but when I got married, that changed. We had to make a living." Ted looked to emulate the success of another local professional athlete at that time. "One of my heroes was Charlie Garringer, who played for the Tigers," he shared. "(Charlie) was a gentleman, never missed Mass, and was one of the greatest second basemen that ever played," he added. "When he finished, he became a very successful businessman." Like Garringer, Marty and Ted used the strength of Detroit as their backdrop. "Marty and I said, we're in the automotive capital of the world, let's use that," he said. Lindsay and Pavolich Sales began. "This is going to be our livelihood when we're finished (with hockey)," he stated. "We're preparing for when we were finished, whether that was going to be two years, four years, or something." In business, Ted learned that being a professional athlete could open doors, but it would take much more than that to close a deal. He applied to his business the tenaciousness attitude acquired in hockey, but admitted that this isn't always the case for those in sales. "Athletes are their own worst enemy," he shared. "Because if I come in, talk to you as a buyer, and don't get a purchase order and then don't come back to see you. Sometimes you've got to call on a guy for three years. They try to test you to see whether you're serious about your business," he added.

By the time Ted was traded to Chicago, Lindsay and Pavlolich Sales had grown enough to support someone full time, which couldn't have come at a better time. "(Red Wings GM) Jack Adams was going to send Marty to the minors, because I formed the Players Association, but he had nothing to do with it," Ted said. "He was going to the minors but the greatest satisfaction in the world he got, was telling Mr. Adams, 'I retire,' and be able to back it up. So he did it. I went to Chicago for three years and came back in the summertime and worked. In 1960, by the time the three years were up, the business had grown to support the both," he added. After playing sixteen seasons in the NHL, Ted announced his retirement from hockey.

Ted shifted his mindset from the fierceness of NHL hockey to the shrewdness of the business world. He also realigned his passions. "My business did," Ted stated when referring to what replaced his passion for hockey. "Whether I'm playing my profession in hockey, when I take my long-term profession, which is my business life, I play and work the same," he said. "I work the same as I played." For Ted, there was only one way to play—tenacious and disciplined. "Our discipline in our profession helped us tremendously," he exclaimed. "I get up at five thirty every morning." Ted's ability to move on with his life after hockey proved beneficial. "Things that were important were important at a very important part of your life, then you move on," he stated. "Life moves on. You become more successful. Our business came along and it was a transition. Our (hockey) career was up here, and our business was coming," he said. Ted credits his successful transition from hockey, not because of foresight, but for another reason. "I loved the game. Nobody loves hockey more than me," he said. "There was nothing good about getting out of hockey I would have played it for another sixty years if I could have. But it wasn't difficult; it was being realistic, common sense. I'm no Einstein, I'm no genius, but I have good common sense," he added.

Ted's career took some twists and turns in addition to his business. In 1964, while doing some hockey TV broadcasts, he was approached by the Red Wings to play again. "I laughed at them," he said. "I'm thirty-nine and I laughed at them. When I realized they were serious, I talked to my wife and she wasn't for it. I talked to Marty and he wasn't for it." Despite the resistance from those around him, Ted decided to lace up his skates again, but made a request to Sid Abel if this were to occur. "I said I want to be the first guy on the ice, at eight o'clock," he stated. "Be out there until nine thirty, shower, dress, and go to lunch with a customer." Ted didn't want his off-the-ice work to miss a beat. After the first round of games in the league Ted realized that his enthusiasm and leadership became contagious and he confronted his teammates. "Who the hell thinks they're better than we are," he asked. "I got the guys to listen and said, 'We can win this whole thing, if we put our mind to it.' We ended up winning the league championship, first time in several years," he added. Following this 1964–1965 season, Ted once more hung up his skates.

In 1977, Ted was asked to come back again by the Red Wings, not as a player but as a general manager this time. "The club had gotten so bad, they figured I couldn't make it any worse," he quipped. "It was a three-year deal, I thought I died and went to heaven." Ted drew a parallel between playing with toys and managing an NHL team. "You know, when you're a youngster, in the gravel pit with your little toys, little cars, and little shovels, and now you're dealing with human beings (instead)," he exclaimed. The NHL must have liked the way he played, as he was voted Executive of the Year. Things turned for the worse when Ted switched hats from general manager to coach at the end of his three year deal. "I coached seven games at the end, at the very end, just before I got fired," he shared.

Now over eighty years of age, Ted measures success in different ways. "One success is that I've got three wonderful children," he said. "I was divorced. I had three children by my first wife but she's dead now for about ten years. I got remarried and then that wife died of breast cancer," he shared. "Then (my current wife) Joanne came along and I am very lucky, she's wonderful. My three children love Joanne; she's a good mother and a great grandmother. We have six grandchildren," he added. "My life is so perfect and so wonderful. I get involved with a lot of charities. Every year I go to Toronto for Special Olympics, where they have a big fund raiser every November. All of these kids got all of these handicaps, but they all got smiles," he said. "You know, we can all take a lesson from them." Ted's charity reaches further for an autism foundation, hosting an annual golf outing every fall. "I got involved with autism because I have a friend that has a youngster that's autistic, and I just wanted to see if I could do something," he stated. "I hope in my lifetime that I'm able to see the cure for autism." Ted's list of charities is rounded off with another personal interest, as chairman of the Alzheimer Society in Ontario. "I took care of my sister for seven years," he said.

Times have changed in the NHL since 1944, when Ted Lindsay first began. "Signing bonuses are more than my whole hockey team made in the seven league championships, all the salaries of those seven teams," he exclaimed. "The guys today never have to work (another) day in their life. Don't just take, you've got to give back," Ted advises, as he shares his simple common sense.

Chapter 14
SHAWN BURR

Shawn Burr was a first round draft choice of the Detroit Red Wings. He played professional hockey for over sixteen years, including stints with the Tampa Bay Lightning and San Jose Sharks. During his last season in Detroit, Shawn helped the club reach the Stanley Cup finals for the first time since 1966.

It is difficult to know what Shawn Burr enjoys more in life, hockey or hilarity. Since donning skates for the Sarnia Black Hawks in 1982 until his final NHL season in the year 2000, Shawn has found a way to do both very well. Originating from Sarnia, Ontario, Shawn played locally in junior hockey until his big break came in 1984, when he was a first round NHL draft pick by the Detroit Red Wings. He had to be patient with his development as he skated between the ranks of the OHL, AHL, and NHL his first couple of seasons.

In 1986, under Red Wings coach Jacques Demers, Shawn came into his game as a center with heavy checking defensively and twenty-two goals on offense. "As a coach and as a person,

I liked Jacque Demers," he said. "(Jacque) played me a lot. I mean, he let the guys play. (We) all hung out together and were pretty close, it was a good kind of core nucleus of players to be around," he added. The core and closeness of this team paid off as they reached the Playoff semi-finals in 1987 and 1988. During his final season with the Red Wings in 1994, Shawn was an integral part of the team that reached the Stanley Cup finals. This was the first time since 1966. Despite the success, things would start to change for Shawn under new coach Scottie Bowman. "He just said that I wasn't his type of player, so I never really hit it off too well with him," he shared. "I kind of knew my days (in Detroit) were numbered. (Also) I had a few injuries, which I never had before." Shawn tore ligaments in his left thumb and was out for surgery. Following the surgery on his thumb, his back became an issue. "I had a little problem with my back, it was just bad luck," he said, referring to the occurrence of the back-to-back injuries. "So then I got traded to Tampa."

Shawn attributes his trade to a combination of the injuries and an incident that occurred during the Stanley Cup finals that year. "I think the biggest disappointment my whole time in Detroit was the Stanley Cup finals," he said. Following the victory against Chicago in the NHL semi-finals, Coach Bowman pulled Shawn into his office and told him that he may not play as much against New Jersey in the Stanley Cup finals. This especially came as a surprise to Shawn because of the fact that he played a lot and considered himself instrumental to their semi-final victories. "We played the first game and I don't play hardly at all," he stated. "And then the second game in Detroit, we play and it's kind of my instance, that famous goal that you think I shot in our own net," he said. Shawn elaborated about this particular play by stating, "What happened was that one of their guys had (the puck) behind the net and I went to go check him. I was getting hooked out in front, so I ripped Niedermayer's stick, kind of pulled it out of his hand and the other guy shot the puck around the boards to Cicarelli. Cicarelli is right-handed and he kind of caught it on his backhand and turned. I'm left-handed, so I'm thinking I'm going to get a one-time shot in the slot," he exclaimed. "I've got two sticks in my hand, so I kind of push the stick away and it goes into Niedermayer's hand. Dino passes it across; Niedermayer jumps in the play, intercepts the puck, skates down, and takes a shot from the blue line. Paul Coffey goes down on one knee, bounces off the inboard, Mike Vernon kind of slipped and Niedermayer shoots it in the net," he explains. "So we go to New Jersey, and I don't play," he said. "Now, I'm like, I'm done with Detroit, but I can still play."

Shawn's trade to the Tampa Bay Lightning occurred during the off-season, which gave him no control over it. "They probably wanted to get me somewhere that they didn't have to listen to me, you know, only twice a year anyways," he said. "They don't play (each other) a whole lot." Later, Shawn discovered that there was more of a reason than what he thought. "Jim Devellano actually called me and said, 'Shawn, I want you to play somewhere that really wanted you, somewhere where you're going to get some ice time.' I had a lot of respect for Jim Devellano. I still think he's the brains behind the whole organization in Detroit," he added.

Under Tampa Bay coach Phil Esposito, Shawn blossomed again and the team made the playoffs. During his two years in Florida he found the warmer weather had a positive physical influence. "As far as my body is concerned, down in Tampa its a little bit better because of the weather and everything," he stated. "So being an older player, you know, I felt good. I played most of the games both years," he added. Despite this reprieve, his lower back began to give him problems by the end of his second year. Shawn was criticized by his peers and sometimes coaches for his less than svelte physique, but felt that it ultimately didn't matter. "They had a body fat tester, so they put this lean muscle mass on the chalkboard in front of the whole team," he said. "I think I was the least amount lean muscle," he admitted. "I'm not blessed with one of the greatest bodies in the world, but I always kind of liked to hit hard. So there was this one guy there that was like six foot five, a kid from out west, and he weighed 260. So we were working out and Phil Esposito comes in and he's like, 'Look at that guy, that's what we're going to build, a team like you.' So we played in our blue and white game in training camp and this kid comes around the net with his head down, and I knocked him out, cold as a cucumber," he boasted. "He was lying on the ice and his tongue was hanging out. They learned that in hockey it was a lot more than just looking good. Sometimes hitting in hockey is just pretty much heart," he elaborated.

Following Shawn's two seasons in Tampa, he was traded to San Jose, but was unfortunately faced with an injury early in the season. This time, instead of a torn ligament in his thumb it was the ACL in his knee. "That was the last year of my contract and they're telling me I was out for the rest of the year," he stated. "Dr. Tangnar, who has done a lot of stuff for the NFL and did Barry Sander's stuff, said that if he could get a cadaver transplant I could be back within three to four months. So I said, let's got for it." Following the surgery and rehab, Shawn came back, but he knew something wasn't right. "I could tell, I never said anything to anybody, but I just knew I was never again 100%," he shared. "So before the end of that year I ended up signing a contract because they thought I was going to get back and be as good as the game I got hurt. I actually had two goals in the game at that time I did it. I signed a three-year deal, which was good," he added.

During the 1998–1999 season, Shawn was sent to play with

the Kentucky Thoroughblades, San Jose's AHL affiliate. "It was probably, since my days in Detroit, the most fun I ever had playing hockey," he shared. "I played the power play, I mean; I never played the power play in the NHL. I went down there and we won ten in a row on the road. We had a rock and roll tour," he exclaimed. "I'm making a million bucks down in the minors and the team payroll is not even that, so I'm making sure when we go out that I'm buying the beers, this and that. I'm like a legend in Kentucky," he joked. "That's the one thing I'll always have and that's what the young players learned from me, is that this guy is thirty-five years old and he's having a ball."

In 1999, Shawn's chance to play and still have fun would move south when he was traded back to Tampa. "I restructured my contract, actually, and took less money," he said. "I just wanted to go back (to the NHL) and play." After playing the first four games of the season, Shawn was informed that the team needed to work the younger players into the lineup and they needed to take him out for a while, which became a serious problem. "I'm not the greatest conditioned guy in the world, so I get out of shape," he said. "They skated me in practice and I actually tore my hamstring. Then I ran into a problem with my back," he added. Following three weeks of rehabilitation, Shawn was once again sent down to the minors, but this time to Detroit, with the Vipers. "My wife was back there anyway, so it worked out," he stated. Poised for a return to the NHL and Tampa, another injury would check his progress. "I sprained my ACL. This guy hit me with a hip check and I knew I had hurt myself," he shared. "So I was hurt for a while." Just when Shawn thought things were bad, they got worse. "Jay Feaster, our general manager, says, 'We loaned you to Winnipeg,' because they were going to make the playoffs," he said. "So I went to Winnipeg and I was hurt and hadn't played much. I get there and Randy Carlisle, the first thing he said to me was, 'You're fat,' and I said, 'Well, so are you.' He said, 'Well, I'm retired,' and I said I thought I was going to be, too, in a couple of months." Now playing in Winnipeg for the IHL's Manitoba Moose, Shawn's words were closer to the truth than he realized. Following a triple overtime loss on the road in Long Island, he decided to end his pro hockey career. "We're all sitting in the dressing room (and) last call has already hit," he said. "There's nowhere in Long Beach to go after the game, so I'm like, 'Guys, let's go to Harry O's in Manhattan Beach.' So we get a limo and we got to Manhattan Beach and we're there until five in the morning," he stated. "We call up to find out what time our plane is and it's a six thirty a.m. bus to the airport. So we pull in and the coach is in the lobby. I went up to my room, went to bed, and never went downstairs," he declared. "I didn't even try. I gave the trainer $500 to send me my clothes and my hockey equipment back," he added. "I was done!" Later that day Shawn flew to New Orleans instead, where he met up with his in-laws to celebrate Easter. "I enjoyed playing the game, I liked being around the guys," he said. "But I like being around my kids."

Shawn already had an idea what the next phase of his life would be when faced with the reality of leaving professional hockey. "I always kept a keen interest in keeping track of financial stuff," he said. Dick Powell, senior vice president at Smith-Barney Financial, knew Shawn's interest and asked him to join the group. "I could do that," he thought. "The hard part is when you come from hockey, everybody just assumes that it's a front to go meet people and he doesn't know what he's doing and he doesn't know anything. Everybody is going to think you're a dumb jock. It's taken me awhile to kind of lose that," he added. In the fall of 2000, Shawn entered a different type of training camp. "I started training camp, again," he stated. "But it was a different training camp, it was at Smith Barney. I started at Smith Barney at the same time training camp started. I figured I'd start right when I would normally start working again," he added. But conditioning for this job was much different than training for hockey; with longer hours, less time off, and exams to maintain, Shawn found some difficulties with the transition. "I still, to this day, struggle with it," he shared. "I have problems working in the summer; I have problems keeping my eyes open between two and three. I napped all the time. The day of the game I'd eat spaghetti and sleep in the afternoon." Another issue Shawn discovered during his transition was his competitive spirit. "I still have problems," he admits. "Like even now in the alumni games, I want to hit somebody. I've played games with the kids, like Mario Golf, I don't let them win. I don't let anyone win anything," he added. "I played in a flag football games two days ago. I hiked the ball and this big bald guy gives me (a forearm shiver) and I bit my tongue and I'm like, 'What are you doing?' and he's just, 'That's how you play the game.' So I get in the huddle and I'm like, 'Are we allowed to hit in this game?' and they said, 'Yeah.' So I hiked the ball, this guy is coming, and I give him a forearm right across the throat," he exclaimed. "He's on his knees and I'm cussing at him. I get back in the huddle and my buddy says, 'You know, this is a church league.' I didn't know what I was doing, you know, he made me bite my tongue."

Despite the difficulties of his transition Shawn discovered some benefits. "This business is competitive," he said. "I think that I'm pretty resilient when it comes to this business. I don't give up just because someone says no. That's what I've taken out of hockey, I'm not afraid to play against good teams. I'll go in against someone with a company that has lots of money and I'll compete. I'm just as prepared as anybody," he added. There were other benefits to getting out of hockey, as well. "Everything slowed down a bit," he said. "I think I got out at a perfect time.

I don't worry about the calipers anymore that measure my body fat," he quipped. "Until I got about thirty I passed off my body fat as baby fat," he said. "My first year, I was 175 pounds at camp and they gave me that protein powder. They told me they wanted me to gain ten pounds, so they gave me this protein powder and told me to mix it with ice cream. It created a monster and I gained five pounds every year now since, but I reached my plateau in retirement," he stated. Playing hockey has also opened many doors for Shawn. "I think it gets me in the door of a lot of places," he admits. "Detroit has been a great city for that. I mean, I can go to other cities and people won't give a rat's ass. People here have been good. My wife always says I'm probably the most famous fourth line player in the history of the Red Wings."

Shawn shared some words of wisdom about the transition from professional athletics back into normal, everyday life. "I think it starts when you're playing," he said. "The most important thing is being involved. Do the autograph sessions, do the charity events, (even) when you're thinking, *Man, I only get one or two days off,* do all that stuff," he advised. Shawn would find out later that this philosophy benefited him many years earlier while he was still playing. "I didn't get traded one time from the Red Wings," he said. "Someone else got traded instead of me because we were at an event and I stayed after and signed autographs and the other guy basically just brushed off a bunch of kids." That player got traded, Shawn was told.

As Shawn Burr continues on the next phase of his life, there is no question he will remain competitive. He funnels this competitive edge from hip checks on the ice into dividend checks for his clients. Not only is Shawn motivated to make himself successful, but the people he services, as well. He takes his new job seriously and states, "I don't consider myself retired. I just moved on from one profession to another."

Chapter 15
JOHN OGRODNICK

John Ogrodnick is a five-time NHL All-Star. He played a combined nine seasons for the Detroit Red Wings organization. In addition, John sported six more combined seasons with the Quebec Nordiques and New York Rangers before calling it quits in 1993. As an offensive threat, John Ogrodnick broke the Red Wings' single season scoring record and at one time ranked statistically with the likes of Wayne Gretzy, Jari Kurri, and Mike Bossy, who are now enshrined in the NHL Hall of Fame.

John Ogrodnick, or "Johnny O" as he was affectionately known in Detroit, subscribes to a very down-to-earth attitude despite his many hockey accomplishments. While raised in Ottawa, Ontario, as part of an Air Force community, the scouting letters began rolling in by the time he was sixteen years of age. Named WCJHL Rookie of the Year in 1978, it wasn't long before the Detroit Red Wings noticed his talent and drafted him in 1979.

In 1980, Johnny's offensive prowess while playing for the Adirondack Red Wings aligned with an unfortunate knee injury to Detroit Red Wing George Lyon and gave him the opportunity to be called up to Detroit in January. Armed with a solid work ethic and strong desire to win, Johnny's impact was evident by the tremendous amount of ice time he received and placement on his first NHL All-Star game in 1981. This began a phenomenal string of five NHL All-Star appearances in six years; a feat few have matched. He experienced his best hockey, skating in many eighty-game seasons, playing a minimum of twenty minutes per game, and scoring thirty-, forty-, and even a fifty-five-goal season. This surpassed Mickey Redmond's previous Red Wing record of fifty-two goals. Johnny credits Red Wings coach Nick Polano for the large amount of playing time, thus larger opportunity to score. "(He) played the heck out of better players," he stated.

At this point in his career, there didn't appear to be much more a professional athlete could want; possessing an All-Star status, a record-breaking season, and a coach who didn't hesitate to ride his better players. Unfortunately, as in many things in life, all good things must come to an end and Johnny wasn't immune to this often unspoken truth. Following the 1986 season, which would be his fifth and final All-Star appearance, the wave of success came to a sudden halt when Johnny was hit along the boards during the fall training camp. "I heard a loud pop and obviously did something to my ankle," he said. "It was an injury common to football players," he added while explaining the inward roll of his left ankle. A downward spiral of his hockey ability would not necessarily come from the injury itself, but from his decision to return from it prematurely. It was the same personal drive that lifted Johnny to his All-Star status that caused him to make a rash judgment despite the skepticism of his doctor. "(It) felt like a noodle," he said. "But it was my mistake, I came back too early. "I couldn't turn, I wasn't playing well (but) I didn't consider my ankle injury the reason for playing bad." As his ice time diminished, so did Johnny's ability to focus. "(My) mind was not into it," he admitted, which initiated a roller coaster ride of confidence that he'd experience for the rest of his career. "If you're a scorer it's all mental, confidence," he added.

Later that season, things began to turn around for Johnny, but the damage was already done. "I was playing well again, getting stronger, and points started coming back, but by then it was too late," he stated. Despite his improvement, Johnny felt the cold edge of the NHL business sword when he was traded to the Quebec Nordiques for the remainder of the season, immediately following their game against the Red Wings. "I wasn't happy going up there," he shared. "The hockey was fun, we had a good team, but not being able to speak French didn't help." Fortunately, Johnny's joy of playing hockey soon overrode his displeasure for living in Quebec when the Nordiques made the playoffs. "That was probably the first time things really got exciting for me in hockey," he said. "We went into Hartford and upset them in the first round of the playoffs. Fans went nuts; it was pretty exhilarating," he added. "We didn't experience that in Detroit because we were a little on the weaker side." Johnny experienced a solid playoff run as he scored nine goals in thirteen games.

The following season, a trade to the New York Rangers occurred around training camp. The next five seasons would prove exhilarating for him. "Very, very exciting," he exclaimed. "We had a chance to meet a lot of celebrities, namely Tom Hanks, Glenn Close, Susan Sarandon, Tim Robbins, Thelma Louise, and Matt Landon." Johnny enjoyed going to movie premieres and met many of the actors who lived in Manhattan while experiencing his own celebrity status that came as a result of a couple of solid scoring seasons and winning the President's Trophy. "New York was awesome," he added.

Though he considered New York life awesome, the roller coaster ride of confidence and limited ice time wore on Johnny. Some games he would only see eight or nine minutes of playing time, but after sharing ice time with Mark Messier, his timing, confidence, and scoring would come back once again. Johnny found himself back on his game and playing more minutes, then for whatever the reason, he was moved back to the time-limited third line and sometimes didn't even dress. "Very, very frustrating," he stated. "Back in the 1990s, thirty-three years old was considered old." The frustration grew deeper as he was in a state of limbo. "They don't play you, and they don't trade you," he said.

Eventually, Johnny signed a contract with the Detroit Red Wings. "I had to scrape and claw to get a small contract in Detroit," he shared. "Unfortunately, I thought maybe Detroit had changed because I was gone for more than five years, and it really hadn't. It seemed like the players were still in control of the team," he added. "(It) might have been different if Scotty (Bowman) was there when I came back."

Feeling like an old stallion put out to pasture, Johnny was sent to the Red Wings Minor League team in Adirondack before working his way back to Detroit. Upon his return, Johnny scored five times during his seven games back. He found himself thrown into the playoffs against Toronto despite having only played a total of nineteen games all season. "Without really playing in two months I was stumbling around the higher tempo (playoff game)," he admitted. Detroit was knocked out of the playoffs in the first round and Johnny was let go. "(Coach) Bryan Murray got fired, (general manager) Dusty McLain got fired, and I'm out of hockey," he simply put. "It's unbelievable how you go from scoring goals in the NHL and all of a sudden you're out of the game. And that's what basically happened," he added. "*C'est la vie.*"

What made Johnny's exit from hockey more difficult was the fact that his New York Ranger line mates went on to play another two or three years. In addition, he realized that the NHL salaries started taking off after his final season in 1993. Johnny used one of his contracts as an example. Having a forty-goal season in New York allowed him to negotiate a contract worth approximately $475,000 a year. A year and a half later Johnny was told by Red Wings general manager Neil Smith that any forty-goal scorer would receive over $1,000,000 a year. "People told me I was a generation too early," he jokingly said.

Following his release from Detroit, Johnny actually thought he might step onto the ice again when he was asked if he was interested in playing for Ottawa. "Sure, I'd love to come up to Ottawa," he responded. "(Just) give me a base salary with some sort of bonuses if I perform." Unfortunately, Johnny's opportunity to go to Ottawa was shot down by their coach. "It's kind of harsh but it's a business," he said. "I wasn't a part of the plan." Shortly after this event Johnny received an invite to play for the Canadian Olympic team, but was not motivated to accept after fourteen seasons of professional hockey. There was something about traveling away from home while being based out of Calgary that just didn't appeal to Johnny anymore, partly because he was still reeling from his last two professional seasons. "The most painful part," he stated when referring to these seasons and his transition out of hockey. "When people ask you if you miss hockey, the toughest, most painful part of it was my last two seasons. In New York, I'd be sitting at the end of the bench, or playing, or up in the press box and then back to Detroit, only playing in nineteen games. (My transition) was gradual but it was frustrating because you knew you could still play and you're chomping at the bit to get out there and you got a coach saying, 'No, you're not going out; you got to sit at the end of the bench.' Those were the most painful times," he admitted. "Those two years and the first year out were the toughest parts as far as when people ask me if I miss playing the game, especially when you know you could still put some numbers on the board," he added.

Johnny took the year off after his departure from hockey and used the time to refocus his life. He decided to pursue a stockbroker's Series 7 License, which came as no surprise since he often enjoyed dabbling with the stock market during his playing days. "One thing I did when I was playing hockey was get involved with the stock market quite a bit," he stated. "Even in New York, I traded commodities out of my house. I've always been intrigued with the business." He decided to settle in the Metro Detroit area and started working for a financial firm that is now called Wachovia. One of the reasons Johnny decided to retire in Detroit was name recognition. "You can open doors with a name," he said. He understood that once in the door he would need more than his athletic attributes to service his clients. Johnny's first order of business was to pass the Series 7 Exam. "Probably one of the most exhilarating times of my life," he exclaimed. "My heart felt like it was pounding through my chest. There was definitely a lot of work involved."

From slap shots to financial indexes, Johnny shared the best part of his transition from hockey. "I'm able to drive my daughters to school," he explained. "Just being around a lot more, not being on the road, living out of bags, family time," he added. "Being more in control of your life, not a coach behind the bench pulling strings and trying to play mind games and all of that shit."

What motivates Johnny now is the same thing that motivated him while playing hockey. "It's the drive to be more successful," he stated. "You just don't want to be a loser, I don't mean a loser like a down-and-out loser, but I'm just saying anything you're doing, you want to win at, you want to do good at." A wave of events, like the burst of the Internet stock bubble and the World Trade Center disaster, made it more difficult for him to initially succeed, but Johnny credits his previous hockey experience for his ability to weather the storm. "Any other Joe Blow may have called it quits and just looked at a different profession," he said. "But the drive and commitment for continuing on, applied from hockey, helped me immensely."

Despite these attributes, Johnny found some difficulties in the business world. "I was too trusting," he admits. "The biggest problem I had getting out into the real world pertaining to business was trusting too many people. People would talk to you, especially in the stock market, and sound very sincere and very knowledgeable but you would soon learn that there's a lot of bullshit," he added. "I'm not saying there are dishonest people but people that would do whatever it took to sell their stock or company. They had their own interest. I'm not smart enough to figure out billion-dollar companies, but I have a lot of competence in smaller companies," he boasts. "I learned the hard way."

As he became wiser every day in business, Johnny still struggled emotionally from his transition out of professional athletics. "You're in your own little shell when you're playing sports," he stated. "You get a nice paycheck, you do your thing, you're a goldfish, you're in a zone," he added. "Hockey, hockey, hockey, then *boom*, you're out into the real world. One of the things I miss the most (is) the exhilaration when you step on the ice for that first playoff game. The fans are going nuts, your blood was flowing, your heart was thumping, it's so exciting," he exclaimed.

Johnny highlighted the biggest successes he's experienced

since playing hockey. "You know what I think the biggest (success) probably for me is that my business is doing pretty good," he said. "For the most part I'm happy with the business part of my life after hockey." In addition, Johnny boasts twenty-three years of marriage to Betty, which he especially appreciates since he knows many players get divorced after their final playing days. Now working out of his house, he has more time with his two daughters, Breanne and Kelsey, and takes great pride in their successes.

Johnny briefly reflected on playing professional hockey during his era. "Back then you had to make sure you had other interests to fall back into when hockey is over," he stated. "You basically needed to stop thinking about the game and move on to other things. You're going to miss it; you just try not to think about it. Brainwash yourself," he added. "Expect a gradual transition."

Now, many years after his fourteen-year professional hockey career, John Ogrodnick has solidly made the transition from NHL All-Star to financial consultant. There is no question that as he continues to apply his acquired attitude of hard work and incredible desire to win, "Johnny O" will continue to find great success in his post-hockey life.

Chapter 16
FRANK TANANA

Frank Tanana played professional baseball over twenty years as a Major League pitcher. During his tenure, the southpaw played eight seasons as a Detroit Tiger and also sported time with the Angels, Red Sox, Rangers, Yankees, and Mets. Frank was a three-time MLB All-Star.

It all began for Frank Tanana at Catholic Central High School in Metro Detroit, where he excelled at both basketball and baseball. As a two-sport All-State athlete his junior and senior years, opportunities to play either sport at the college level were abundant. "I had over 100 offers," he exclaimed, but baseball proved to be his favorite. "My first love was baseball," he said. "It was what I was always better at and excelled in." Following Frank's high school graduation in 1971, at seventeen years or age, the California Angels agreed that he excelled in baseball and drafted the left-handed pitcher, making him the thirteenth player picked overall. He was faced with the decision of turning pro or going to college. "I chose Duke University, where I was going to go (play basketball), had I gone," he stated. But the Angels offered Frank a contract he couldn't refuse. "It was one of those deals with baseball, at that time, what was a sizeable bonus," he said. "I think it was $60,000 to sign. Just the opportunity at that level and that was really what I wanted to do," he added. "I was okay in school, I'm no dummy but I just loved to play and this gave me an opportunity to focus on athletics."

As Frank became eighteen years of age that summer his long professional baseball career would begin, but it didn't start the way he had planned. "I had a bad arm when I signed and thought it would get better but it didn't," he said. "I missed that whole summer with a bad arm." His disappointment was expounded by the current NCAA rule pertaining to his amateur status. "That was a hard year because back then you couldn't play another collegiate sport. Once you were pro you were done. And they've since changed that, but at that time I was screwed," he stated. Frank was sent to Idaho and his disillusionment with turning pro grew even deeper. "I hadn't done anything and couldn't even pitch," he shared. "So I sat around there really for an entire season. And all through that, of course, you're taking injections, trying to get rid of the pain, and nothing seemed to work."

The following season Frank's circumstances suddenly changed when he reported for training camp. "I went to camp the next year for spring training and had to see the doctor," he said. "And then for whatever the reason, I took a shot and bingo, something popped in. Everything just got well." The following season would prove to be even better for Frank as he played AA ball in El Paso, Texas. "One of my best pro seasons of any level," he exclaimed. "I was 16 and 6 and led the league in strike-outs with a good ERA. I just really started to progress to the stature I thought I should have been and believed I could get to," he added. Later that season, Frank progressed to AAA ball in Salt Lake City, where he threw a one-hit shutout his first game. In

September, Frank finally got to go to the place that he wanted and would be for the next twenty years. He pitched in four games and completed the Angels season. For the next seven seasons Frank rode a wave of accomplishments in California and was part of a one-two pitching punch with Major League's Hall of Fame pitcher, Nolan Ryan. "I had my glory years with the Angels," he said. "I was on top of my game, won a lot of games, played on three All-Star teams, leading the league in strike-outs and ERA at one time and shutouts. Just pitching very, very well," he boasted. "Then I hurt my arm again," he said. "I went through a lot of innings early in my career. I would probably average 260 innings my first five years. I also had a lifestyle that wasn't conducive to keeping the body in real good shape," he admitted. "I worked out but certainly wasn't what you would call dedicated to my profession. I ran a lot but as far as weights and that, I really didn't do much. I had a drinking problem; I was drunk all the time," he shared. "I since have learned that one of the greatest deterrents for recovery for muscles is alcohol and no wonder I was sore all of the time because I was drinking all of the time and it took my arm longer to recover," he candidly admitted.

Working through his injured elbow, Frank decided to change his pitching style, which proved to be very unpopular with the Angels' management. "I really didn't know how long I could throw hard and continue in the big leagues so I made an adjustment to become more of a finesse-type pitcher and ran into some difficulties with management," he stated. Following the 1980 season, Frank was traded with two other teammates in a big blockbuster deal to the Boston Red Sox. After spending just one season in Boston, he found his way to the Texas Rangers, where he would spend the next four years. Frank recalls that first year in Texas, "I had a terrible year; I think I lead the league in losses, 7 and 18. I started giving up more runs and needed more help from my team, where before I could just strike people out. We weren't a very good ball club," he added. He hung in for a few more years until a managerial shift in 1985 would propel Frank into a very good situation.

In June of 1985 Frank was traded to the Detroit Tigers and commented on the transaction by stating, "(It) really worked out well because the Tigers were the World Champs, they had just won the World Series the year before and I ended up falling into a very nice situation. Solid team, good guys, they knew how to play the game and played to win and I was a recipient of that. I was the same guy but, you know, better cast, you get better results," he added. Frank sported solid results in Detroit, which was highlighted by a fifteen-win season in 1987. He would remain with the Tigers for eight seasons until the organization took a different direction in 1992. "We parted ways," he said. "I was thirty-nine years old and they wanted to go young. I understood that." Lucky for Frank, a buddy by the name of Jeff Torborg was managing the New York Mets and inquired about his interest in playing. "I went to the Mets as a free agent in '93 and with three weeks to go they traded me across town to the Yankees and I got three starts and finished out there," he shared.

Frank found himself at spring training for the California Angels the next year, but realized his days would be numbered despite his desire to still compete. "Ten days or two weeks or so into camp they decided to go another direction and gave me my release," he said. "After that, the phone didn't ring. That's all she wrote, that was the last of it. I was forty years old, the career was over."

At this point Frank had played professional baseball for twenty-two seasons and though grateful that it lasted that long, he struggled with the realization that he was totally done. "It was wonderful, no question, a great life," he said. "You've got the mentality, I'm in shape, I want to compete, I want to play, I know

I can bring it to the table, I know I can be a positive factor to any organization just by my character, my lifestyle, my experience but you know, I had a 7 and 15 record with the Mets," he admitted. "That's a hard sell, there's a forty-year-old guy and look at his last year. I understood that but that was tough for me. But it was one of those things where my story is going to be majorly different from a lot of guys due to a transformation that took place in my life halfway through my career," he stated with a Cheshire grin. "(It happened) halfway through my career, back when I hurt my arm again and (was) consumed, especially from a worldly sense. That's your life, that's your livelihood. So with my second arm injury and the fear of being out, the fear of being twenty-five years of age and out of the game was a very scary proposition as far as identity because I was a Major League star," he added. "That's what I was in my own mind. You're on top of the world, you're a star. Everybody is carrying your bag, you're in the newspapers, you're in magazines, and you're on the cover of *Sporting News*. When that was almost taken away from me (along with) a couple of other things that happened; a teammate of mine got shot and killed in Gary, Indiana, one night after a baseball game, Cathy and I had just gotten married so there was a change going on there," he said. "And then I met a guy who was our chaplain by the name of John Warehouse. Just his personality, his character, his persona, the way he lived his life is different than really any other guy I ever met," he exclaimed. "So he just kind of won me over, we became friends. He showed me some scripture (and) I began to go to Bible studies. I began to get an idea of what Christianity from a Biblical sense is all about, not from an organizational sense, not from a religion, but I just began to differentiate and see and finally come to an understanding for what it means to have a relationship with God through faith in His Son, Jesus Christ," he shared. "Because of my life and the way I was living it, finally coming to the point of committing myself, like a man does to a woman when they get married, God calls for that same sort of commitment to receiving His Son, the Lord Jesus Christ. So I did that on November 6, 1983, and became what the Bible terms and what people here phrase, 'Born Again.' I became a follower of Christ and began to look into the scriptures."

Frank's newfound faith during the middle of his professional career gave him a newfound perspective on baseball and life. No longer would he view things in the same matter nor have the same priorities. "Christ gave my life direction, a new direction," he said. "It gave my life a new purpose. Jesus Christ transplanted baseball as my priority." He elaborated on how this new perspective affected his transition from professional baseball and stated, "Ten years later, after I had had a chance to grow and have Jesus Christ and the Word of God prove to be true, and live a very blessed and unbelievable life, not only in baseball but in relationships with my wife and my kids and my coworkers, and being involved with the community, and trying to help other people come to this wonderful relationship that I had with Christ; baseball became not less important but put in its proper place," he explained. "So since I'm now worshipping Christ and living for Him, when baseball is taken away, when it was done, I had grown more to understand it was going to be done. You don't *need* that stuff, you're thinking a whole different way and it's phenomenal. You used to *want* and *need* and now you don't," he added.

When faced with what to do after the final pitch of his career was thrown, Frank turned to divine guidance and gained insight. "God began to show me what's important, His Word and people," he stated. "People are what's important, not your job." Following this guidance, Frank became more involved with people and had a focused purpose. "To build and to grow and to invest in them all for the purpose of staying strong scripturally, biblically, and spiritually," he exclaimed. Now as a worshipping member of Highland Park Baptist Church the obsession of baseball has been replaced with a fervor that still maintains a hint of competitive spirit. "I began to be very comfortable speaking to people about a relationship with Jesus Christ and it became my passion, it became my zeal," he said. "There's a tremendous competition for the soul on a spiritual plane. What better thing to be about in life than competing for the souls of men," he shared. "I'm still pitching and that's what's cool. I'm not throwing balls, I'm now throwing the Word of God at people." In addition to his pitching for souls, Frank did admit to finding another outlet for his competitive spirit. "I've got the drive, I've got the competitive edge, so I picked up golf," he said. "I enjoy golf, it's a challenging sport, which I like as an athlete. So I kind of put them juices into that."

Frank threw no curve balls when he spoke of the void left by his departure from baseball, but was quick to mention the platform that the sport provided. "You've got to feel like you're somebody because that's what you were made to do, especially a guy, as an athlete," he stated. "And to have that taken away, there is emptiness, there is a void. I can't pinpoint a time but there are moments where you miss what you had. I mean, you miss doing what you're very good at and you can't do anymore," he shared. "Once you get that celebrity status, playing twenty years in the Major League, you establish a name. I've got a name here in the community that people, especially if they know sports, would recognize. I'm able to use that amazing platform."

Having had the luxury to live in many places throughout his lengthy baseball career, Frank elaborated on his decision to remain in Metro Detroit. "So at the end of my career when people say, 'Where are you going to go and live?' I said, 'I'm not going anywhere, Detroit is my home and why would I leave an area where everybody knows me and I can talk to them and get into places?'" he stated. "(In addition) the kids were of high school age and they didn't want to go anywhere, so it was perfect. I'd be foolish to leave."

Frank now lives his life with feelings of gratefulness and gratitude because of the many things he has been able to experience up to this point in his life. "My life has lived on such a high plane because of Christ that it's like everything is a bonus, everything is wonderful, seriously," he said. "I mean, my relationships, my marriage, my life with my kids, church involvement, and the opportunity to speak to thousands for Christ and just be a bold witness for Jesus," he added. Other than spending time with his family and playing a few rounds of golf, Frank walks his talk by boldly speaking about his faith. He uses his days as a professional athlete as the platform and extols how a spiritual conversion halfway through that career provided a whole new perspective and priority on life. If Frank Tanana can apply the same competitive spirit and self-discipline he had during his twenty-year Major League career to his current calling of "competing for souls," he's going to have a good chance of winning.

Chapter 17
RICK LEACH

While attending the University of Michigan Rick Leach was voted Big Ten MVP, football's College Player of the Year, and All-America in both baseball and football. He then boasted a ten-year Major League Baseball career representing the Detroit Tigers, Toronto Blue Jays, Texas Rangers, and San Francisco Giants.

Rick Leach was an athletic thoroughbred. He was a three-sport All-State athlete in high school, a two-sport All-American athlete in college, and ultimately enjoyed a ten-year career as a professional athlete. Rick was the standard of his time for students who played multiple sports. His drive to excel was phenomenal and unprecedented in many ways. He was also a natural-born leader. All he wanted to do was play sports, and he did, which made his eventual departure from athletics that much more challenging.

As a result of his father's influence, Rick's transition into sports was quite easy. Often, he could be found on the sideline of his father's baseball and football games and practices as a kid.

This exposure at such a young age motivated Rick to become a three-sport athlete at Flint Southwestern High School, where acquiring athletic honors came all but second nature to him. As a three-year starter in football, basketball, and baseball, he earned All-State honors for all three sports by the time he left high school. Some considered him the most talented athlete in the state of Michigan and deservedly so. The Philadelphia Phillies drafted the left-hander shortly after his high school graduation, in 1975, but Rick was not ready to commit to only one sport and continued to search for a college that would support this endeavor. He turned down the Phillies' reported six-figure offer.

The University of Michigan's maize and blue was already present in Rick's athletic bloodline as his father and uncle both played baseball for the university. This history made it even more refreshing to discover that head football coach Bo Schembechler was tolerant of his interest in playing multiple sports, so Rick became a Wolverine. While attending Michigan he earned countless athletic honors and was considered one of the finest athletes in the university's history. As a four-year starter at quarterback, Rick broke many single-season and career records, was named first team All-Big Ten three times, a three-time Heisman Trophy candidate, received multiple Player of the Week awards, was a Big Ten MVP, and named first team All-American as a senior.

Arguably, one of Rick's greatest college football moments came during a much-publicized game against his celebrated counterpart, Joe Montana, who had just led Notre Dame to a national championship the season before. Rick was seriously injured during practice the week before the game and was doubtful to play. Despite this injury and trailing 14-7 at halftime, Rick still played and led Michigan to a 28-14 victory. "He is the greatest football player I have ever been associated with," Schembechler proclaimed that year.

As a baseball outfielder for the Wolverines, Rick won the Big-Ten Batting Championship and was named All-America, making him one of the few athletes to become All-American in both baseball and football. It was easy to say that Rick Leach was the cream of the crop and at the top of his game, but he was torn when it came down to choosing a professional sport after college. Rick decided to hold off on any decision until after the NFL and MLB drafts, which allowed him to see how things might pan out.

In May of 1979, Rick was a fifth-round pick of the National Football League's Denver Broncos. One month later, he was a first-round draft pick of Major League Baseball's Detroit Tigers. Rick mulled over both offers even though his heart was leaning a certain way. "I loved football, especially college football," he said. "When you're used to playing in front of over 100,000 people every home game and seeing everybody and the fans and going around these stadiums all around the country. Baseball is a whole different mentality and a whole different mindset." Unfortunately, when it came to pursuing his passion for football the Denver Broncos had a different idea. "They wanted to take a look at me as a defensive back," he stated. "I wasn't interested, I didn't want to really waste their time or mine because I've been a quarterback all my life. If I can't make it as quarterback, I'm not going to try to make it as a defensive back," he added. Rick signed with the Detroit Tigers and received a $125,000 signing bonus, which was one of the largest of its time.

As an extremely intense young athlete, Rick learned that he needed to change his attitude in order to play professional baseball. "I was always known as a tremendously competitive athlete," he said. "I'm going balls out; I'm going to play as hard as I can. There's not a lot of contact in baseball, but when you get a chance for it, I certainly didn't shy away. I was playing with a football mentality," he exclaimed. "You can't have an attitude like I had with football when you had a whole week to get ready for one game. I'm going into every (baseball) game with that kind of mentality and I said, *I'd better learn to back off.* You're not playing every week, you're playing everyday," he added. At the age of twenty-two, with money in his pocket and a professional baseball career ahead of him, Rick also learned that there was another side to professional athletics. "(I learned that) there is a lot more than just playing ball," he exclaimed. "Having to make financial decisions, investment decisions, and tax decisions. I'm going to have to hire some people to kind of figure out where I should put my money. My dad and some U of M people helped me."

In 1981, after two full seasons with the Tigers' Minor League teams in Lakeland and Evansville, Rick was called up to the Majors. He remained with the Tigers until 1984, when he signed with the Toronto Blue Jays as a free agent. Rick played for the very talented Blue Jays until free agency moved him to the Texas Rangers in 1989. The following season Rick played with the San Francisco Giants, but he was released in 1991 during the last cut of spring training. "Of course, my hope (was) another team will pick me up," he said. "It didn't happen. That's when the transition and reality starts to hit. At that time everybody that's getting cut loose is trying to find a job and (other baseball organizations) may be getting calls from a hundred guys," he added. "I put up some pretty good numbers and played pretty well but had some other issues that I'm sure some might want to take a look at, and they were uncomfortable with some of those things. I understood that," he stated. "The only thing that bothered me through the transition was that I was making pretty good money at that point. I wasn't an everyday player in baseball,

I was a role, utility type, but I was known as one of the tops at what I did and got paid accordingly. When I'm trying to find a job, it just became irritating when some people would say, 'We're not going to pay that kind of money.' I tried to eliminate (the money) and said, *I'm just at the point now that I want a job,"* he added. *"I don't necessarily care what I make, although I want to be fair, but I don't have to make X amount,"* he exclaimed. Rick's realization of being done with professional baseball sank even deeper over time. "After you go through two, three weeks and nobody is calling and you're trying to just hook on and say, let me play AAA and show you what I can do and you're not getting responses, I mean pretty much reality is hitting, that's it, man," he said.

In one sense, Rick was fortunate because he still received one-third of his salary that season because of the time frame he was cut. "At that point I just decided to take the time, it was pretty devastating all of a sudden realizing that it's over unless something quirky happens," he said. "I wanted to stay in shape, work out, and just relax with my family. I had a young family at that point and with the money I had received, I knew I could do that, so I decided to take the summer off and just get my feet on the ground and see what was going to flush out. Reality is hitting me, too, and what the hell am I going to do," he added. Rick played a lot of golf, especially in charity golf outings. He didn't passionately pursue any other career leads because he held on to the outside hope that something was going to work out so he could still play, but that unfortunately didn't happen. "As we got into summer and it starts to get to fall, my wife starts to ask me, 'What are you going to do?' It was obvious that it wasn't going to work out with professional athletics anymore. I had to start trying to figure out what I was going to do and how I was going to do it. We talked between us about going back to U of M and finishing my degree. A lot of guys who played one sport (in college) would take a lighter load during their season and bulk up or take more hours when they weren't, (but) because of playing two sports and the amount of time, I never had that opportunity," he exclaimed. Going back to school and taking college courses proved to be more difficult at thirty-four years old. In fact, it proved all but impossible. "When I got back (to college), all the technology advances had started to really come to the floor and I was technologically bankrupt," he shared. "I had no clue, I was overwhelmed. After being there a short time I just told my wife, it was almost like taking a foreign language to me. I was driving myself to where I was having my own internal issues because it was just too damn hard for me. I'd rather start trying to use some of my contacts and people," he stated. "I'm thinking it's going to be a major, major struggle just to get through it. I don't want to devote that kind of time and effort and go through the internal issues, because a lot of them were my own," he added. "I'd been gone so long; I didn't have access to tutors and study tables and stuff like you do when you're on scholarship there. I'm starting at what I would call an elementary level going back in when these guys are at a graduate level. At that point, and at my age, I just didn't want to spend that time and effort," he said. For the second time, Rick left the University of Michigan. Looking back at his years as a collegiate student-athlete, Rick pondered on how his first experience in college could have been different. "The one thing I wish could have been different was that in some ways I wish I could have gone to college without the burden of the athletic part of it," he stated. "Without the burden of practice, film work, I mean I was a gym rat. I did whatever I had to do to get my homework done and then watch another hour of film on my next opponent in football or going down to the IM building and hitting more weights. I was so darned tired (from) doing two sports," he said. "At that time, I just wanted to get through school. I always had it in my mind that unless I had a severe injury I would at least have an opportunity to play professional. That was going to be my ticket. This is my preparation as a professional athlete. So I did what I had to get through school instead of bearing down like the majority of other people," he admits. "I have regrets, I didn't at the time, but now as I'm older and see stuff, I'd like to go back and change, but I can't."

Following this attempt to finish his degree, Rick started to tap into his contacts. "I started searching around and talking with people, and trying to find some opportunities that I thought I could fit in," he said. "At least if I'm going through a big learning curve, because there's going to be a big learning curve in the real world, at least I'm going to get paid for it and see the result of what I'm going to go through to do it," he thought. Rick discovered that the curve might actually be larger because of his previous status as a professional athlete. "I knew a lot of people weren't going to be fond of me being there or think that I'm given opportunities or things, preferential treatment," he stated. "Here's another one of these jocks thinking they own the world and coming in. I was bound and determined to prove I'm going to pull my weight."

Rick finally saw the results of his efforts and got into a commercial printing business as a sales representative with some ownership opportunities. With a financial stake in the company but no real business experience, he learned that he was blind as to how things should work. He also learned that things were not financially adding up. "Things weren't making sense to me," he said. "But I wasn't smart enough or (didn't) have enough financial background to really confront (anybody) on it. I was responsible for bringing in a new bank (and) new opportunities just through relationships that I had and after meeting with my partners, going through the financial (information), I learned almost right out of the gate, and it was probably a good experience, although detrimental, that guys can put anything on paper," he shared. "Anything that goes out of here is supposed to have three signatures for X amount or above, (but) there's checks going out of here for more than that amount," he stated. "I started having questions and things weren't making sense to me." Rick consulted with some of his successful business contacts who were part of his University of Michigan alumni family and shared the issues that made him very uncomfortable. He became livid as his business-savvy friends shared their thoughts on his situation. Fortunately, Rick had a provision in his partnership that allowed him to pull his money and get out within a certain time frame. Unfortunately, as he was trying to get answers and to the bottom of what was really going on, that time frame lapsed. "To make a long story short," he said, "I got my eyes opened in a hurry because we came to a stalemate on disagreements. I'm (one of) the owners and I'm paying my things out of my personal money and they're paying their stuff out of corporate money. So I had to go through a year-and-a-half, two-year court battle to eventually get my money back. I learned in a very painful way (that) by the time you pay court costs, attorney fees, deposition fees, everything else, nobody wins," he shared. "It was tough on me, tough on my family, going through a lawsuit. It was a nightmare. It was a real eye opener. I was devastated," he added.

At thirty-five years of age, Rick experienced his first hard lesson during his transition from professional sports. "Bad start. Very, very bad," he stated. "As an athlete you go through a lot of mental changes. Number one, the thing that you loved and enjoyed all of your life is gone." As a professional athlete now back into normal, everyday life, Rick's education was not from any textbook or university, but directly from the school of hard knocks. Though he was a tremendously gifted athletic leader for most of his life, Rick learned that to be a leader in business, he would have a lot of learning to do. "The main thing was I knew I'm not qualified or sophisticated enough, especially in a business sense, to be going in on an ownership kind of thing," he said. Despite the negative impact of this event Rick expressed great appreciation for the help of his Michigan alumni family. "I've always had access to the Michigan alumni family, which I couldn't stress enough what a wonderful opportunity it's been."

Now equipped with the realization of his limits for business, Rick ventured in a different direction and worked as a salesman in the insurance industry for seven years. Following those seven years, he worked another seven years in the trucking industry, mainly on the sales side with Ford, Chrysler, and GM. "I had to basically start at the bottom and learn on the fly," he stated. Consolidations, cutbacks, and financial issues ultimately caused the demise of the trucking company and his job in sales. He once again found a steep road to finding the appropriate employment and stated, "People told me that their positions (are) more entry level for high school or college kids starting out. They don't want to pay you health benefits, along with salary," he added. "Everybody's cutting back."

Rick had lukewarm responses to job inquiries and was uncertain of what to do next. Fortunately, his athletic past would once again come into play. Not in the form of the contacts he developed from playing, but in the form of a longtime battle fought in court by the Major League Players Association. "Through things that happened with ownership and the union, the Players Association fought and won a big battle in court," he shared. "I was able to reap the benefits and get large sums of money over four years that I never counted on coming." With slim pickings for employment, the financial windfall came at a very good time. "Fortunately for me, my wife is working and successful, and I was smart enough to sock a majority of what I made and put it away," he said. "I've got a (baseball) pension plan that I could start collecting right now if I wanted to, but the longer you wait the more it builds up. The kicker with our pension is that once you take it, whatever the number is, that's it for the rest of your life, just a flat amount," he added.

As a result of the MLB Collusion Settlement, things financially improved for Rick, but he experienced some difficulties as he looked to refocus and eventually find employment again. "I decided to take some time off," he stated. "A year or two years possibly (but) getting back into things turned into four years. The last two years were a big struggle. I thought I could go back into the network of various people I met over the years, but door after door was getting closed in my face. It was getting frustrating (and) it was tough on my family," he added. "It was really difficult in the fall and winter, when you're cooped up inside and that's why I still held out hope that certain things were going to happen in the business world." Eventually, Rick's hope developed into a reality when he landed a position as a sales representative with Detroit Pencil Company, an office products distributor based in Troy, Michigan. Once again, tapping into the network of the University of Michigan family paid off. "There was a U of M alumni named Tom Parkhill that I've known for a long time," he said. "When I first came out of high school he was someone that supplied one of my first summer jobs through U of M (and) a summer jobs program for football players. He was a longtime GM executive and took an early buyout and is currently at (Detroit Pencil Company). He approached me and wanted me to come take a look and said they dealt with office supplies and office furniture. My first reaction was, selling pens and pencils, you've got to be kidding me!" he admitted. "At that point I was semi-desperate to desperate and went ahead and took a shot at it. It's amazing how blessings happen to us because I don't think I've ever had more fun and enjoyed it more," he exclaimed. "I feel so blessed, because everything that I wanted in my afterlife of athletics is coming to fruition now. It feels almost exactly like when I was in a team atmosphere," he added. "We have people in various roles and functions at our company that all of it has to be put together and work for us all to be successful. Things are going so well and coming so fast and furious that it feels like it's playing Ohio State every day. That's a great feeling for me; the adrenaline, the enthusiasm. (I'm) waiting to get up at the crack of dawn each day and get after it again. The passion and the drive and the enthusiasm, I can apply all of the things that I did to athletics to what I'm doing now and that's a great freedom!"

Nowadays, in addition to his job, Rick has great passion for his family and is especially enthusiastic about his three boys; Michael, Matthew, and Ryan. He spends his time religiously attending countless athletic and educational events with Angela, his wife for well over twenty years. You'll often find Rick's parents, in-laws, and other relatives in attendance, as well. He puts heavy emphasis on his kids' education and frequently reminds them of its importance. "I'm trying to impress upon them to get where you guys want to go, do everything you can in school," he said.

Rick did not complete his college degree, but in many ways his education has stretched far beyond what a classroom could've provided. The characteristic traits developed from athletics have proved instrumental when overcoming what he educationally lacks. As with any thoroughbred attempting to do something different from what he was bred, Rick has had his difficult moments. "I had a lot of difficulties when I got done playing baseball," he shared. "It was hard to try and find something that had the (same) enthusiasm and excitement. It's just so hard for so many athletes that when you go through that process, some are prepared to go on to what I call the afterlife after athletics, but I think an extremely large number aren't sure where to go," he added. "You just have to put so much time and effort and drive and enthusiasm (into) being successful to stay at that professional level that to try to prepare to go to something after that is extremely difficult for some people, and I was one of them. I just focused on what I had to do and didn't think of when that day would come because I was trying to prolong and extend it as long as I could."

Ultimately, the drive and tenacity that Rick learned directly from sports have benefited him well as he continues to rise and face these difficulties head-on while accepting nothing short of the best for himself and those around him. Rick feels grateful for the opportunities that have developed because of playing sports. "In a lot of ways I feel blessed and lucky that my dreams were able to basically come true," he said. "I beat the odds and wouldn't want to put money on me doing it every year. I always had the belief, but when I look back, I think, *Man, (I was) one of the very lucky few.*" Rick Leach is not the only lucky one, for as he continues to apply his drive to succeed in other aspects of his life there is no question that those around him will become a lucky few, as well.

Chapter 18
JIM NORTHRUP

Jim Northrup played Major League Baseball for twelve seasons, eleven of which with the Detroit Tigers. As a professional he was known for his elite batting skills, that included two eight-RBI games, two grand slams in a single game during consecutive at-bats, and three grand slams in a single week, as many dubbed him Mr. Grand Slam. In 1964, Northrup was MLB Rookie of the Year and became a World Champion with the Detroit Tigers in 1968.

Jim Northrup was born and raised on a farm near Breckenridge, Michigan. His father was insistent that he get involved with sports, and Jim credits him for most of the baseball that he learned. When Jim was too old for Little League, it was his father who bought bats and balls in order to form a Legion League team for the local sixteen- and seventeen-year-olds. This was the same team that traveled to Battle Creek to play in the Legion Finals against what could be considered a classic country boy versus city slicker team rivalry. "We damn near beat those hot-shots," he recalled.

As a well-rounded athlete at a rural high school in St. Louis, Michigan, Jim excelled at football, basketball, baseball, and track. Following his high school graduation, he decided to attend Alma College on a basketball scholarship, but soon discovered that the college needed him for more than basketball. As a pre-med student on this 750-student campus, Jim discovered that if you were any type of athlete, the school wanted you to play as many sports as possible. He found that his goal of becoming a medical doctor would be difficult to achieve, not necessarily because of the strenuous curriculum but because of the demand the school placed on him as an athlete. Jim's athletic involvement at Alma began to compound when he discovered that his chemistry professor was also the baseball coach. He also discovered that his basketball coach was the track coach, and then found out that his baseball coach also coached golf and football. In all, Jim stated he would've earned a total of seventeen athletic letters if he'd stayed all four years at this private institution. As an example of how easy it was to make any team, Jim simply asked the football coach, "What do you have to do to make this team?" The coach, who happened to be Jim's baseball and golf coach, simply replied, "Find a uniform that fits you." Jim eventually went on to become a small college All-American in football. Despite his accomplishments, this very coach kicked him off the baseball team his junior year, ironically, around the same time that he discovered professional baseball scouts had been interested in him since his Legion Final game in Battle Creek. Jim's father apparently discouraged a very interested White Sox scout from signing him then and there because he wanted him to attend college. Jim had no previous idea of this event.

Jim opted to leave college after his junior year at Alma College and played in a baseball league in Saginaw, where he would pitch, play outfield, first base, and bat fourth in the cleanup position. That same year he attended a Detroit Tigers invite tournament and went six for eight, with eight RBIs. When asked by a Detroit scout to come upstairs and sign a contract, Jim boastfully exclaimed, "There is a small problem, I didn't get a chance to pitch," he stated when referring to the tryout. In no uncertain terms, the scout explained to Jim that there would be no more pitching if he was going to sign with the Tigers. He swiftly retracted his outspoken concern, when he discovered that this scout also signed Al Kaline, Willie Horton, and Mickey Stanley.

While joining the Tigers' Minor League team in Decatur, Illinois, Jim faced something that he'd never faced in baseball before, a left-handed pitcher, but this soon proved not to be an issue. "It didn't make any difference to me which hand you pitched, just throw it over the plate and I'll hit it," he exclaimed. Jim's lifetime batting average is higher against left-hander pitchers than right. In 1964, he was called up to the Majors, won the batting championship, and was awarded Major League baseball's Rookie of the Year. During his many years as a professional athlete, Jim was a part of many personal and team accomplishments, which includes leading the Tigers in hits, RBIs, and homeruns at key times, causing many to dub him *Mr. Grand Slam*. As a key member of the Tigers team, he eventually won a World Series Championship in 1968.

Despite his achievements, things turned bitter for Jim following his eleventh season in Detroit. "(They) sold me," he stated with a sharpness of anger in his voice as he referred to his trade to Montreal and then to Baltimore, which became especially disheartening because of the fact that he joined the Orioles after the September playoff deadline, thus unable to join them in the World Series. As a result, he often joked amongst his teammates about breaking their last player's legs in order to activate him. Jim soon took a liking to his new environment, but found it difficult to make it work. "I loved Baltimore," he exclaimed, mostly because of Oriole manager Earl Weaver. But Jim was not making enough money to own a house in Detroit and Baltimore, and commuted back and forth in order to spend time with his kids. Despite his affection for baseball and Baltimore, the emotional drain of this commute would prove to be the beginning of his transition from professional baseball. The frustration of having a family in Detroit while playing out East was difficult as indicated in his attempt to spend time with his children. "I would drive and get them and I'd drive them back home and then get on an airplane and fly back," he explained. "I just got tired of it, it was too much," he added. "I was gone almost the whole season from home. I pulled a lot of muscles, (was) tired of being away from home, it was just time for me to get out," he said. "You have to quit sometime, enough is enough, and I felt it was time to go home. It was very difficult to leave the game because it was what I knew how to do best. I didn't want to, but the time came when I had to, and there was nowhere to go," he added. "In today's market I could have lasted two or three more years just as a pinch hitter, but I saw the end and (figured) I'll just have to find something else to do. I always knew there was life after baseball," he added.

Jim was given the opportunity to become a baseball coach as he faced the reality of exiting professional baseball, but admittedly realized that it wasn't the right career for him. "I'd make a pain in the ass of myself," he admits. "Agents have conditioned (their clients) to not pitch more than six or seven innings. Crybabies, six or seven innings, pitch counts. I faced better pitchers in AAA and Puerto Rico than there is today," he added. "I just wish I was playing for eight million dollars a year." Jim referred to an event with former Tigers teammate and pitcher, Denny McLain, as he illustrated the difference of the pitchers from his era and the present day. Standing next to McLain on the mound when their manager approached for a possible pitching change, he heard McLain bark, 'There ain't nobody in that bullpen better than me, now why don't you get the hell out of here and let me finish this game.' Jim elaborated on how he would handle his pitchers if he were a manager. "I'd say, there is no pitch count," he said. "I'll decide when you've had enough and when you haven't. If you don't believe me, any of you get in trouble and you think you're going to get jerked I'll make you pitch until you give up a hundred runs," he stated. "I don't want your agent calling me; in fact, I don't want him anywhere near our ball club. If you're going to cry go see the general manager. I don't want to see your kids in the locker room or your wife. We have a place for them, they don't belong in the locker room." Jim expressed his final thoughts on how he'd handle his team and said, "Agents and players don't run my ball club. If you don't like it find another ball club." Sadly, Jim understands that a manager would get in trouble for this kind of talk today. He also learned that a coaching salary would not comfortably support his family. "They paid on the average $12,500, then you go down to the minors, ride a non air-conditioned bus and play with a bunch of snot-assed kids, for $12,500," he stated. "My taxes in Birmingham (Michigan) are $6,000, now how the hell am I going to live on 12,500 bucks, there was no way I could support my family on $12,500."

Having played during an era where it was common for professional athletes to work in the off-season, Jim's transition into other work was already in place. He spent many of his off-seasons selling insurance, doing public speaking engagements, and landed a job with a cattle company out of Fowlerville, Michigan, two years prior to his baseball retirement. In

Fowlerville, Jim worked for Bill Britain, founder of Hoover Ball Bearing, and Bob Bolin, who knew the cattle business inside and out. "The two smartest people I've ever met," he claims. With 100-200 head of Black Angus cattle, 2500-3000 commercial grade cattle, two slaughtering plants, and three feed lots, this was not your everyday ma-and-pa operation, but a full-fledged industry. Jim sold tax shelters, wrote a prospectus for vegetables, and eventually hit harder times with new tax laws that changed profitability for the cattle business.

Foreseeing the blight of the cattle business, Jim's associates sent him to run a coalmine in Georgia. Understanding enough to know this could be a lucrative opportunity, Jim paid a visit to the mine with his wife and met the operation foreman. At their initial meeting, Jim couldn't help but notice the .357 Magnum strapped to the foreman's hip, which prompted him to ask, "What's the pistol for?" As the foreman was explaining the occasional problems he had with the miners, Jim already knew what he was going to say to his associates back home and cornered Bob Bolin upon his return. "Bolin, this little northern white boy's going down to Georgia, put a .357 on his hip, and get killed… I ain't going," he exclaimed. "(Needless to say), I had to find something else to do."

A downward spiraling cattle business, having had enough of insurance sales, and a disinterest in coal mining would lead Jim to an opportunity with the Detroit Caesars softball team, which was owned by Mike Illitch. "We had the best softball club money could buy," he stated. "We were the Yankees of softball. (Illitch) went out and bought all of the best softball players he could buy, adding Norm Cash, Mickey Stanley, and myself," he added. "They wouldn't let us play much, we were there to draw fans, and we knew it."

Ultimately, a chance to become a manufacturer representative with an old teammate came to fruition. Bill Freehan, Jim's roommate from his days with the Tigers, had already established a manufacturer representative business with his father and partner and asked Jim to join the team. Despite his enthusiasm and willingness to learn, he soon found that it took a couple of years to make any money. "When you sell a product it takes two years to approve and be sold," he stated. "You have to wait two years to get your money."

The financial adversity Jim faced tested his character, but he remained confident and the difficulties motivated him to achieve even more. "I've always been confident in my abilities to do something, not arrogant but confident," he said. "Once I decide to do something it will get done. I've always been this way," he added. "When people would say, 'You're never going to do this, you're never going to do that,' I'd say, 'Oh yeah, how the hell do you know?' My desire to win is stronger than anyone else," he exclaimed. "I just want to (succeed) and whatever it takes that's what I'm going to do. If you don't like it just get the hell out of my way," he stated. "I'm not going to be stopped; I don't care what you think!" This inner drive is why Jim was such a great baseball player, and why he would continue to achieve off the field.

It is this will to win and succeed as a team that Jim misses the most since retiring from professional baseball. "I came up from the minors with some great players," he said. "We knew how to play the game, we were a damn good ball club," he added. "We would've, should've, could've won in 1967, then we won it all in 1968. It was a team that was collectively together for four to five years in the minors, then we all came up. We wanted to win, we knew how to win," he shared. "The camaraderie was there, our families starved in the minors and we grew up in the majors. We had been playing together and we liked each other. A lot of them were like brothers; Gates, Willie, Earl Wilson, Lolich, Freehan,

Stanley, we all came up as a bunch of kids. There was no dissension on that ball club."

Jim feels that today's professional athletes are different, especially when it comes to salaries, but he understands that they always have one thing in common; their professional careers eventually end. "I'd tell anybody there's going to be life after baseball," he stated. "I don't care how much money you have, you got to do something. You can't sit around, what you going to do when you're all washed up at thirty-five, thirty-six, thirty-seven years old, if you make it that long? So you have 40 to 50 million in the bank, what you going to do, sit in a rocking chair and watch television all day? The minimum (salary) when I played was $8,000, then it went to $10,000. The average player was making $36,000 when they retired," he added. "I didn't play for the money but I'd sure as hell loved it," he joked.

Now over thirty years after his final days as a professional baseball player, Jim reminisces of the glory days and his thoughts of having baseball infamy. "Everybody thinks I should be in the Hall of Fame," he said. "I probably wouldn't have made the Hall of Fame even if the DH was around. My body fell apart, I was pulling muscles, I could only run three-quarter speed," he added.

Jim Northrup is now far from the challenges of going head to head with pitchers, chasing fly balls, and dealing with pulled muscles. He still routinely goes to his office in Southfield, where has worked for many years since departing from the game. Jim hasn't faced the daily grind of a professional baseball schedule in a very long time, but now faces the discomfort of carpal tunnel in both wrists, no doubt assisted from his activities while playing. Despite the fact that he is now confronted with more adversity off the baseball diamond than on, there is no question that this legendary Tiger, Mr. Grand Slam, will continue to find a way to hit another home run and win in the game of life.

Chapter 19
ROGER MASON

Roger Mason played professional baseball for fourteen years. His modest beginnings started with the Detroit Tigers organization in 1981 and blossomed to pitching in the World Series for the Philadelphia Phillies in 1993. Known for his ability to come in and pitch in a pinch, this man of large stature quietly played for seven different Major League teams throughout the course of his career.

While attending a small rural high school in northern Michigan, Roger Mason not only became a standout by his physical stature but by his achievements as a multi-sport athlete, as well. The six-foot-six, 220-pound athlete received All-State honors in baseball, basketball, and football at Bellaire High School but was only offered one college scholarship, for football, which actually would've been his second choice if he'd have his way. "What I wanted to do was play baseball at Central (Michigan University) but they weren't interested at that time," he said. So with limited options, Roger donned the red and white uniforms of Saginaw Valley State College (which is now a university), excelling at both football and basketball. A baseball team didn't even exist at the school until the later part of Roger's college career. "It was a club sport the first year and the following year it became a varsity sport," he stated. "There was a bunch of us that got together and we went to the (Athletic Director)," he went on to say when explaining the reason for the development of the team. While attending Saginaw Valley State, Roger lettered in basketball all four years, football his first two years, and baseball his last two years, but his passion remained with only one. "It was always a dream of mine to play professional baseball, but boy, the path I was on sure didn't look conducive to it," he said. "I went to a school that didn't even have baseball to begin with; there weren't any scouts coming around or anything."

After completing college, Roger and his then pregnant wife, Terry, decided to go back to Bellaire, where he would spend the summer playing in a fast-pitch league in neighboring Elk Rapids. "We had college guys playing from the area," he said. Later that summer, Roger caught word of a possible opportunity as the Tigers and Royals hosted a tryout camp in Traverse City. "I went to that, and kind of tried to talk to the scout after I got done throwing but he didn't seem real interested, so I came home and figured that was it," he said. "(The Tiger scout) called me about a month later and asked if I was serious about wanting to play. I told him I was and he said, 'I'll send you a contract and send you down to Spring Training.' That's how I started, I went to Lakeland (and) unbelievably, I made the team," he exclaimed.

Roger spent his first season at the Single A level in Macon, Georgia, until the following season, when he was sent to Lakeland. "That's where everything kind of started to turn around," he stated. "It's still A ball, but it's a step up." Unfortunately, Roger had to step down from the mound halfway through the season as a result of a shoulder injury, for which traditional treatments of cortisone shots, ice, and ultrasound did not prove effective. It wasn't until Roger began to exercise on an unusual machine in the training room that things got better, and then some. "The coach had just one of these real cheap (pieces) of exercise equipment in the training room," he said. "After about two weeks or so, my arm started getting stronger and I could throw again." He finished that season, continued on his exercise routine, and was immediately sent to AA ball when he returned the following spring. "I did the exercises and all of a sudden they're clocking me in the low 90s," he exclaimed. "I went from the high 80s to the low 90s and all of a sudden, I went from suspect to all of a sudden, *who is this guy?* That's why my shoulder got hurt because it was weak," he added. "The next thing I know, Fourth of July, I was in AAA (ball) in Evansville." His team went on to win a championship.

In 1984, Roger's career would really take off. "So in 1984 I go to the big league camp and talked to Sparky (Anderson). I was one of the last guys sent down," he said. "When spring training was over, (Sparky) said, 'You're going to be one of the first guys we call up.' So I was in Evansville waiting for a phone call. It ended up being the end of the year (and) I got called up." In the fall of 1984, Roger would officially become a Detroit Tiger. "They brought six of us up," he said. "The Tigers started out that year 35 and 5. (They) had Morris, Petry, and Wilcox, that's all they needed at that point; Rozema, they were just so solid," Roger stated, but he still had an impact. "From the very first day, apparently, I set the team record for longest relief appearance, eight innings," he boasted. "That was extraordinary! Unfortunately, I was ineligible for the World Series because with the September call up, you had to be up before the roster expanded," he shared.

Roger spent that winter pitching in Puerto Rico and received discouraging news of a trade from his agent. "So I went through all of the emotions in Puerto Rico," he stated. "All of our friends were there in Detroit, in the Tiger system." Roger would experience the roller coaster ride that is sometimes associated with professional sports when he discovered that one of the players involved with the trade balked, so he reported to the Tiger training camp. Unfortunately the trade eventually went through at the completion of camp. "I came back, went to spring training, got traded to San Francisco, and spent the rest of the time in the National League," he recalls.

An untimely injury and the desire to still compete had an effect on Roger's next couple of seasons. "At the time, when I came out of spring training, I was really throwing the ball well," he said. "For the first month, month and a half, I was a league leader in a number of different categories. And (then) what had happened was I hurt my back, which kind of altered my mechanics and led to me hurting my elbow," he added. "The mechanics never got fixed so I kept putting more pressure on the elbow." Driven and not wanting to give up any ground, Roger more or less pushed himself to a breaking point. "I wanted to pitch, I had waited a long time to get there and I was having some success. I got to a point where I just couldn't (pitch)," he admitted. "One thing led to another and I ended up having surgery on my elbow. It took some time to recover from surgery, to really rehab back to where I was." Placed on the disabled list, Roger would spend the rest of his season rehabilitating and found himself back with the AAA team located in Phoenix the following year. "I was on a Minor League contract, again. I was throwing the ball really good again but ended up getting released from the Giants (organization) at the end of the season. I went from there to Houston and spend a year with the Astros, most of the time in Tuscon (AAA ball)," he shared.

Roger's revolving door career continued in 1990 but some assistance from a previous Minor League connection proved beneficial in his quest to play. "I got released out of camp with Houston and ended up with a tryout with the Pirates," he stated. "They invited me over there because Jim Leyland was there, an old Tiger guy. I guess he had a soft spot for ex-Tigers because he wasn't that far removed from Detroit at that time," he said. Once again playing AAA ball, this time in Buffalo for the Pirates organization, Roger got called up following his appearance on the AAA All-Star team. "From that point on I was with the big leagues," he said. "(The Pirates) were in the middle of three years in a row of winning their division (and) I ended up having one of the best stats they have for relievers, inherited runners and runners scored," he exclaimed. "I had inherited twenty-one runners and only one guy scored. It was just one of those extraordinary things. I'd come with the bases loaded and miraculously get out of it."

As a Pirate, Roger also experienced his first Major League play-off. "It was Atlanta's first year," he recalled. "Then they won all these championships in a row so I mean the tomahawk chop and all that stuff, it was just extraordinary. I remember going out in game five, and we were winning one to nothing, and I was out on the mound in the bottom of the eighth. I came out with two outs and Ron Gant was up, and he was like an MVP candidate that year. He ends up popping it out and I pitched the last inning and ended up getting the save," he boasted. "Just standing there in Atlanta, I had to step back and look around. It was so extraordinary to have 50-some thousand people chopping and chanting in unison, and I was right in the middle of it. It was just like one of the most extraordinary things ever for me," he admitted. "That was an incredible highlight."

Following the 1992 season, Roger was, once again, released,

but he took it in stride as he had learned to be quite resilient. "I ended up signing with the (New York) Mets in the winter and got traded to San Diego just after Christmas. So I started with the Padres and we went on a road trip right before the All-Star break. The first trip was supposed to be Philadelphia, New York, Montreal, and back to San Diego but the first day was a rain-out," he said. "The second day was a double-header (and) it ended up being the longest double-header in history. It ended at 4:41 in the morning. I pitched in both of those games." The day after this phenomenal feat Roger's professional life would change once more. "I got to the ball park, it was just before the game (with Philadelphia) and the manager called me into his office. So I walk in right before the game and the general manager is in there. They go, 'Well, you've been traded.' And the obvious question is to whom, and they say, 'To the Phillies.' So I went outside, took off my uniform, packed my bags, right then, right there," he said. "I said good-bye to all of my friends, walked down the hallway about 100 yards, and put their uniform on and played."

Despite another transaction in his professional life, Roger soon realized that there was a silver lining to his move. "I go to a first place team (and) that fall I ended up in the World Series," he stated. "I ended up having a chance to pitch in four out of the six games. It was just an extraordinary experience just to play," he added. "There was all sorts of media, there was so much media we couldn't even get on the field and stretch. It was foul line to foul line," he shared. "As a matter of fact, Terry and I went to Australia that winter on a baseball mission trip and there were people in Australia who knew who I was because they (had) watched me in the World Series."

From the indescribable experience of pitching in a World Series to being recognized on the other side of the world, Roger's life as a professional baseball player would take a sudden and unfortunate turn. At the beginning of the 1994 season he was traded to the New York Mets, where he would briefly remain, until the Major League Baseball strike. "We ended up coming home (to Bellaire)," he stated. "We were having a great time at home because I hadn't been home in (basically fourteen years). So we were having a really good time but I was still throwing and I did something to my arm, I have no idea (what). All of a sudden my arm started bothering me and it got to the point where I couldn't pitch. It was keeping me awake at night, I just couldn't sleep, nothing was comfortable," he added. "So I ended up calling the general manager at New York and I told him what was going on and he said, 'Well, let's get this taken care of.' I wasn't under contract at the time because there was no contract (but) they took care of me," he shared. After arthroscopy surgery and almost two years of rehabilitation, Roger realized that he had approached his final days on the mound. "I had like a two-week period where I really felt like I could throw again and they wanted to see me so I pitched four games in one week and it was done after that," he said. "There was nothing left, it was everything I could do to get the ball to the plate. (I) just ended up coming home."

Fourteen years into his professional baseball career, Roger now faced a transition from his craft, and he ultimately came to grips with the reality of his situation. "It was just one of those things, like this isn't going anywhere," he said. "I was thirty-seven, it's not like I was twenty-seven, and so it was just time and everybody knew it. The age thing, you're at a point where you can only go so far. There are a couple guys right now like Clemens and Randy Johnson doing what they're doing but they are by far the exception," he added. "Part of the transition was real easy because I had been in different places where guys would come into the clubhouse or you would talk to them in the stands, they would come to the game or something and you knew they were having a tough time with it because they still felt they could play. I knew I couldn't play," he admitted. "Plus, being up (in Bellaire), you're four hours away from Detroit. You're just so far removed from the baseball life, it was over so it was just time to move on. That part of the transition was real simple," he stated.

The positive attitude and resilience Roger learned from being a journeyman in professional baseball assisted in his transition. "I had a lot of perspective," he said. "So my perspective is I just enjoyed it. I remember one time warming up in (Los Angeles). I had come into a game because somebody was hurt (and) I'm sitting there on the mound, because you have all of the time you want when somebody gets hurt. So I'm out there and I'm throwing and I start to throw this pitch and that pitch and I start laughing and I'm like, *What am I doing?* I'm only going to use two pitches here for the next hitter or two, so I said, 'Let's go, I don't need all this time.' I just had fun most of the time."

Despite Roger's positive attitude, the financial reality of being out of professional baseball and the timing of his exit would prove difficult. Caught in a contractual loophole because of the fact that he was not under contract when his final injury occurred, he shared the downside of his transition. "Basically, for two years I (only) got expenses," he shared. "I was in Florida and Terry and the kids were up here, so you still have all the other expenses without a salary. So for two years I really didn't get paid," he stated. "So when I came home I hadn't been paid for two years, so now it's time to move on. I was actually in the middle of the highest salary I had ever had, which was $500,000 and I only got just a little over half of that (because of the strike). At the same time, we built the house for Mom and Dad and that's when everything was paid because we've wanted to do this forever," he added. "We talked about this when we first got married, that we would help her Mom and Dad out with remodeling their house. So it's like, the position that we're at, it was not a big deal because the following year we'd finally be able to put a little bit of money away for us. Well, that never came."

Like going to a favorite pitch on the mound, once again, Roger's positive attitude would help him pull through. "That's just not the way it worked out," he said. "But see, through my whole career, like one of my life (Bible) verses was, 'everything works together for good.' When you've played with seven different Major League teams, and all the Minor League teams, and the eleven out of fourteen years you played were in the Minor Leagues, it's like, You know what, Lord, You've got a purpose and a plan here," he shared. "So when the transition was being made, it's like that verse is going to apply. It didn't change because my occupation changed."

In addition to his financial adjustment, Roger experienced another difficulty. "The hard part was when God started really working on me," he said. "See, the Bible talks so negatively about pride. We talk positively about pride. You need to have pride in what you're doing, you need to have pride in this and that, but scripturally, pride is always a negative thing," he stated. "So anyway, I guess I've always considered myself a nice guy, so how much pride can a nice guy really have? Well, you start to find out. God shows you. It's like, okay, you've got to provide for your family, so one of the first things I did was (work at the) Laminates Factory, as they were hiring. So I just pitched in the World Series a couple years ago, now here I am in a factory working," he exclaimed. Things got even tougher for Roger and his family when the factory had its first lay-offs in years. "So that's when Terry and I opened the restaurant," he said. "It was a small pizza joint outside the corner of town." They eventually sold the business, leaving Roger, once again, looking for a job. "Another year (of playing) and I wouldn't be landscaping right now," he stated as he reflected on his next job.

Once again, Roger drew from his positive nature and stated, "Coming from northern Michigan, playing at Saginaw Valley, not having a real baseball team, and then getting signed at a tryout camp. God opened up those doors for me," he said. "I really, realistically, should have never been there and I always knew that. And you know I can't be upset or bitter or anything about any of the other stuff that happened after that. I could have been working at Laminates (Factory) twenty years before that. God gave me a chance to play baseball, but I always knew, the Bible when it talks about Job, Job says the Lord gives and the Lord takes away, blessed be the name of the Lord. The Lord gave it to me and when it was taken away, it's like, blessed be the name of the Lord," he stated. "God has moved me into just different things in my life. The finances weren't there to just play golf the rest of my days because there is work to be done. I don't mean work in that sense, I mean work in the sense that everybody, whether you play professional athletics or not, God has put His finger on everybody. Everybody has gifts and everybody has a calling in their life," he added. "It's just that most people don't fulfill what it is that God has actually called them to do. I have at least got a little bit of perspective on that, I think, to where it's like I know that baseball comes and goes, athletics come and go, even if guys play in their forties, it's still (temporary), but life goes on and at some point, when we face the Lord, it's like, what did you do? It's like, well, Lord, look at my World Series ring. It's not like, gee, in the Bible you'll see the requirements for having a World Series ring. On top of thoroughly enjoying doing what I was doing I was just providing for my family. You just move onto another phase in your life," Roger exclaimed.

Roger has discovered the next phase of his life in the form of full-time ministry. He currently heads the Northern Michigan

House of Prayer, which hosts prayer walks, vigils, and Bible studies. In addition to this calling, he enjoys another benefit of being out of professional baseball. "The greatest thing about (being out of baseball) was being at home with the kids," he stated. "Just being around them that was the best stuff, being here with the kids."

Different than many front-paged athletes who face post-athletic financial crisis, it wasn't an issue of gambling or drugs that devoured the large sum of money Roger made in his final year. It was an issue of generosity. In fact, despite the longevity of his baseball career, it wasn't until his last few years that his income would even be considered lucrative by professional sport standards. Coming from a humble community, given the opportunity to play professional baseball for so many years, and now back to his humble beginnings, Roger Mason would find a way to be grateful and happy no matter what curve ball life throws his way. Recently faced with his wife, Terry's, battle with cancer and the financial and emotional strain that that accompanies, Roger digs deep into his faith and trust in God's plan while once again proving his ability to step up to the mound and do his best. Not necessarily possessing a household name from his days as a professional athlete, Roger's life will ring even larger because of the positive impact he will have on others. This large-statured man, who once impressed his opponents at the plate while standing on the mound, is now leaving a large imprint on the small community from which he came. Leave it to Roger Mason to step in and humbly give it the best that he can while being grateful for the opportunity.

Chapter 20
DAN PETRY

Dan Petry pitched for the 1984 World Champion Detroit Tigers. As a Major League All-Star his career spanned thirteen seasons while playing for the Detroit Tigers, California Angels, Atlanta Braves, and Boston Red Sox.

While attending El Dorado High School in Placentia, California, Dan Petry made a decision that would ultimately influence the next nineteen years of his life. "I made a decision back in high school, after my freshman year, that I just wanted to play baseball," he said. Even though he had interest in playing other sports, it was this decision that allowed Dan to begin honing his skills to a razor-sharpness, and it really came as no surprise. "It seems like I was always taking a ball and throwing it up against the garage," he stated. "Driving my parents nuts with the constant *boom, boom, boom.*" Often watching the Major League game of the week hosted by Curt Gowdy and Tony Kubek, he ironically envisioned himself as a Detroit Tiger since the age of ten. "I can remember playing the '68 World Series against my neighbor and I was the Tigers," he said. "I had everybody's stances down perfect, although I had a rough time being Mickey Lolich because he was a left-hander." Commenting on the ribbing he often took for acting out his baseball fantasies and vision of playing in the big leagues, Dan added, "People used to make fun of me because I always did dream and had some confidence that I could go on. I took a lot of heat but always, deep down, had that drive."

Growing up ten miles from the California Angels' stadium may have made his outward dream of becoming a Tiger more difficult, but fate and irony eventually came his way. "It worked out funny that I followed the Tigers very, very closely," he quipped. In 1976, before his eighteenth birthday, Dan's lifelong dream became a reality. The All-State high school graduate, who just came off a State Championship in the spring and intended on pitching in the fall for California State University, was drafted by none other than the Detroit Tigers. Picked in the fourth round, Dan was unable to legally make his decision to play professional baseball because he was still only seventeen years of age. After initially rejecting Dan's desire to turn pro, citing college as the reason, his father woke up the next morning and told his son, "You've been dreaming about this all of your life." Dan's father called the Tigers' scout back, explained the change of heart, and allowed him to sign the contract.

Beginning with rookie ball in Bristol, Virginia, Dan would progress through every rung of the Tigers' Minor League ladder over the next three years until his entry into Major League baseball in 1979. "I was able to take my time and play for some great managers," he said. One of those great managers included current Tigers manager Jim Leyland, who was Dan's coach when they won the A ball championship in Lakeland, Florida. With the winning ways ingrained through his early professional years, winning a World Championship in 1984 as a Tiger was almost to be expected. "I'd been around for eight years already, so I had the opportunity to play with a lot of those guys for a long time, so we were very close to say the least," he stated. "You dream about making it to the big league, but you also dream about winning the World Series," he added. "I played with Alan Trammel, Lou Whittaker, Lance Parrish, and Kirk Gibson for a number of years." The bond they developed became very evident as they progressed together to the top of the baseball world.

Not long after his World Series Championship, Dan's baseball world took a turn for the worse following his 1985 All-Star appearance; he experienced an elbow injury and surgery that shortened his season. "It was the start of a downhill decline," he stated. "You wonder if you're going to be able to come back and be the same pitcher that you were prior to being hurt. I don't think I ever made it fully back, velocity-wise, but we won another championship in '87, a division championship," he added.

Despite his nine seasons and many successes in a Tigers uniform, after the 1987 season the splintering of the team began, and Dan was not immune. "I got traded to California," he said. "I didn't want to go back and have to play in front of family and friends again, so I went out there for two years, then came back to the Tigers, which was really nice. I had to work hard for this (trade)," he added. "I signed a Minor League contract and had to make the team." Despite accepting a step down in his contract, after posting fourteen years of professional pitching under his belt, Dan was not yet ready to dwell on the thought of life after baseball, even though it was in the back of his mind. "I still wanted to play and everything," he said. "But you just start gently thinking about what you might want to do or direction you might want to go in." He attributes this futuristic thinking to sound advice given by one of the most influential people in his life. "I remember all the time Sparky (Anderson) would always tell people that this isn't going to last forever, and he planted a seed and something stuck with me that, eventually, this is all going to be done, and you're going to have to do something (else)," he shared. Little did Dan know that that *something else* wouldn't be far off.

In 1991, Dan remained with the Tigers for half the season before getting traded to the Atlanta Braves, "Which was probably the worst six weeks of my life," he said. "I couldn't wait to get out of there." His wish came true shortly thereafter, in the form of a trade to the Boston Red Sox. "That's when I kind of said, okay, the writing is on the wall," he stated. "I was miserable, the kids were starting school, so it was like, I've had enough of this crud. Here I am traveling around the country, and you don't see your family." Dan wrestled with what to do and despite the strong sentiment he had about baseball from the previous season, he returned to spring training the following season and tried out with Pittsburgh after being released from Boston. "(I wanted to) just give it one more shot," he exclaimed. "I already had it in my mind that I was going to play AAA, but I got to spring training and got released, and that's when I was like, okay, that's over with." Dan's agent presented an opportunity for him to play overseas but he turned it down. "I said no. I'm done, finished, I don't want to do it," he said. "It's time to get on with the rest of my life and figure out what the heck (I) wanted to do. I had no idea what I wanted to do," he added. "I didn't know that I'd be playing baseball all of this time, I didn't go to college. I didn't know what I wanted to do other than coach." At thirty-three years of age, Dan understood that baseball is what he did for most of his life so a career in coaching seemed like a natural transition. He referred to a conversation Sparky had with him about this very subject. "Sparky called me in the office and told me, 'When you're playing days are done, make sure you come back and see me because I'll always have a job for you,' (but) I made the decision at that time that I wanted to be with my family," he shared. "I didn't want to go off and start in the Minor Leagues coaching and working my way up. Would I have loved it? Yes, I would have been perfect at it, but I made the decision to stay home and let that go."

Knowing what he wasn't going to do at this point in his life, Dan was left with the decision of what he was going to do. He called upon his baseball contacts, mentors so to speak, and looked for guidance. "I started going back with the contacts I got to know and contacts with baseball; for instance, Bill Freehan," he said. "He made a transition into a very successful career after playing baseball. I got with those guys and was like, how do I do this, tell me what I should be doing." At thirty-three years of age, Dan would put together his very first résumé. "I went to a guy that told me how to put some ideas down on paper," he stated. "I went to the library and spent a lot of time formulating things to put down," he added. Even though Dan was outwardly networking and building a résumé, he still inwardly wrestled with thoughts of playing. "(You're) thirty-three, you're a young man, you feel great, you're thinking, I can still pitch, I still feel strong," he shared. "But at the same time, I played seventeen years (including) the Minor Leagues. I mean, how long can you go? You always know it's going to end sometime."

Three months after his final release from baseball, Dan's connections paid off and he landed a job. "A friend of mine, his brother was vice-president at this company and they were looking to hire somebody," he simply put. "I've been there ever since. I'm in sales and we work for the distribution arm of International Paper."

Things were really falling into place for Dan; he was able to remain at home in Metro Detroit with his wife and kids, he had a solid post-baseball career, he was even able to coach baseball as an assistant with his boys' high school teams, but his full transition from playing was not complete. "I remember for several years when spring training would roll around, I still got a funny, weird feeling," he said. "Your internal calendar or something. It took a long time to get over and those first couple of years out was really kind of hard. It's still there, just not as strong," he admits. "I still want to play, like right now, my arm feels great. I know I can't play anymore, but I want to."

Now in his late forties, the extent of Dan's playing is for fantasy camps and charity softball games. He appears on the radio regularly during the Tigers' season and spent time assisting in pre- and post-game television broadcasts of the Tigers' 2006 World Series appearance. Doing these broadcasts as well as coaching his boys helped Dan work through the difficulty of his emotional transition from playing baseball. "That's where I got my fix. You're still involved with the game, just at a completely different level," he shared. "You're not walking away from the game; you're still very much involved, (and) working with young kids."

It's now easy for Dan to draw parallels from playing baseball. Whether it is in the role of a spouse, the role of a father, or in the role of a salesman, he puts it pretty simply. "You're just performing," he said. "When you're successful, it's a great game. When you sell something, that's a great game, but when you don't, when you're a failure at anything, it's not a whole hell of a lot of fun," he added. He also uses the same motivation that he applied in baseball to motivate him in life. "I guess, more than anything, it's not wanting to ever, ever be embarrassed and that's where I try to take that into business," he shared. "What I do now is try to be as prepared as I possibly can with a customer, because you never want to be embarrassed by them asking me something, or they knowing more than I do."

Working over fourteen years for the International Paper Company, twenty-four years of marriage to his wife, Chris, raising two boys together, and occasional radio and television work with the Tigers completes Dan Petry's résumé since playing professional baseball. Not bad for someone who never completed a résumé until thirty-three years of age. Despite the underlying yearning to still play, which has appeared to diminish over time, Dan uses his confidence and the lessons learned from baseball to better himself. He has taken his game to the next level, to the next phase of his life, and now pitches to corporate representatives. He uses his status as a former professional athlete to inspire the young athletes and tells them, "As much passion that you have, thinking I'm going to play in the Major Leagues, or the NHL, or NFL, or NBA or whatever, it's not going to last forever," he said. "But chase that ring, because you can only do it when you're a kid." It's good to see that Dan Petry has followed his own advice.

*